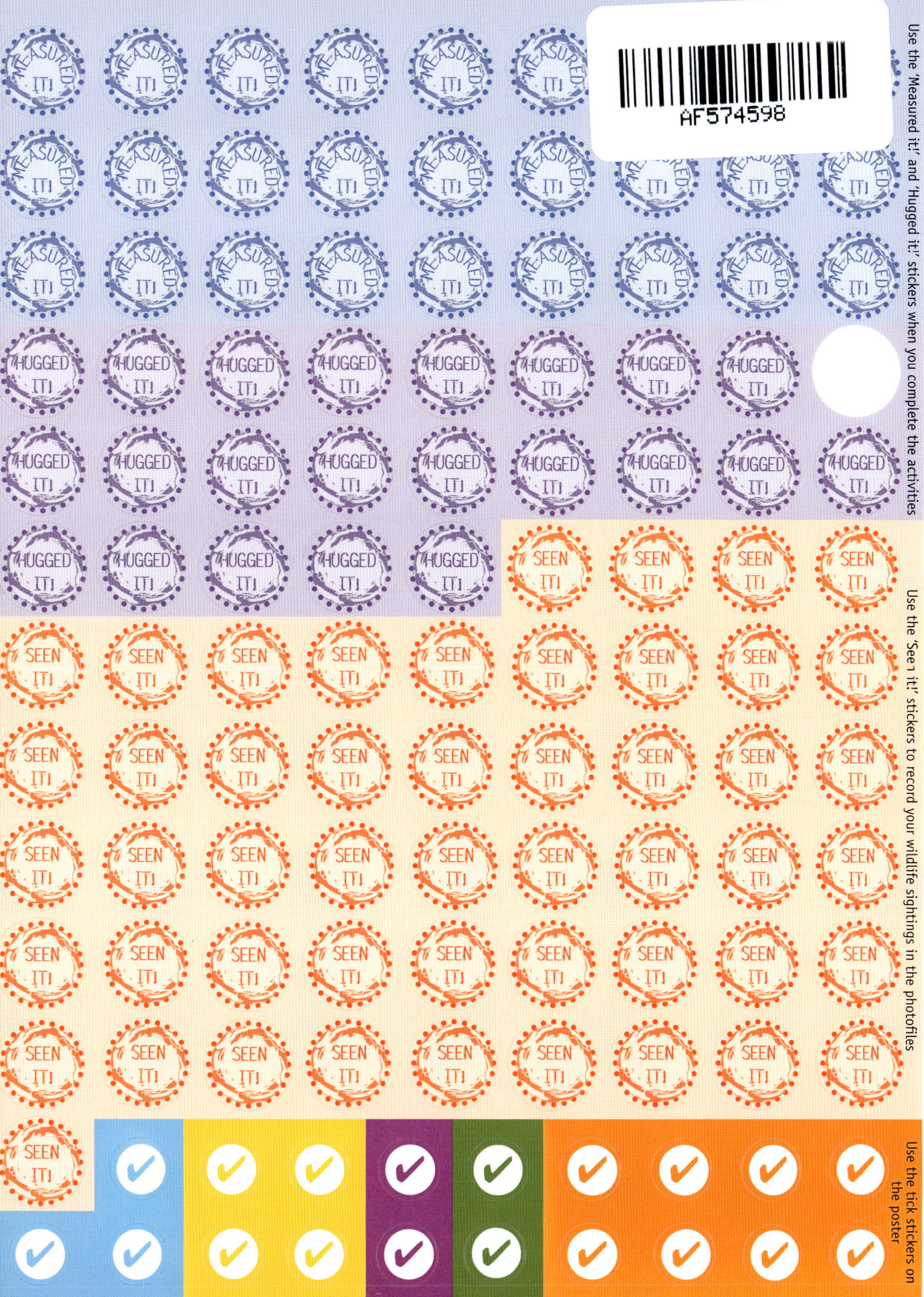
AF574598
MEASURED IT!
HUGGED IT!
SEEN IT!
Use the 'Measured it!' and 'Hugged it!' stickers when you complete the activities
Use the 'Seen it!' stickers to record your wildlife sightings in the photofiles
Use the tick stickers on the poster

tree detectives' handbook

Camilla de la Bedoyere

First published in 2008 by Miles Kelly Publishing Ltd
Bardfield Centre, Great Bardfield, Essex, CM7 4SL, UK

This edition printed in 2009

2 4 6 8 10 9 7 5 3

Editorial Director Belinda Gallagher

Art Director Jo Brewer

Assistant Editor Carly Blake

Designer Carmen Johnson

Production Manager Elizabeth Brunwin

Reprographics Stephan Davis, Ian Paulyn

Woodland Trust Conservation Advisor Fran Hitchinson

Assets Manager Bethan Ellish

ISBN 978-1-84810-009-1

Printed in China

British Library Cataloguing-in-Publication Data
A catalogue record for this book is available from the British Library

Made with paper from a sustainable forest

www.mileskelly.net
info@mileskelly.net

The publisher would like to thank the Woodland Trust for their valuable contribution to this book.

CONTENTS

Once you have identified a tree, mark it off in the tick boxes to keep track of what you've seen.

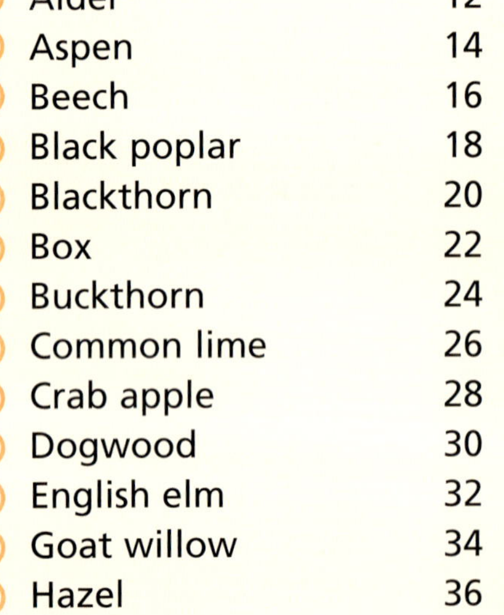

OVAL

LONG

HAND-SHAPED

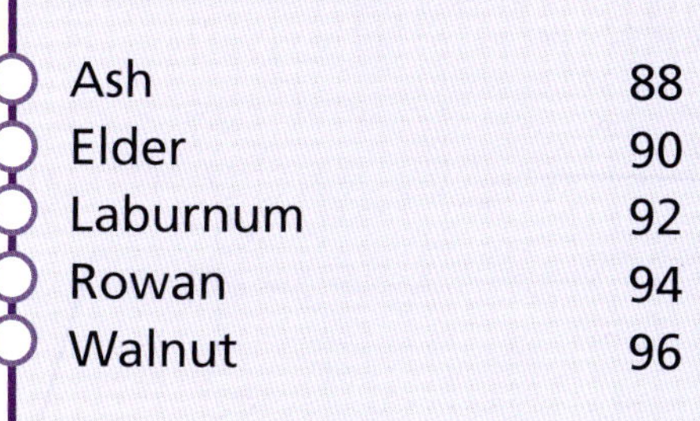

COMPOUND

NEEDLE

Foreword

WE OWE A LOT TO TREES.

They warm us, shelter us and provide us with building materials. If it wasn't for trees, this book wouldn't be printed on paper and you wouldn't be reading it!

The very least we can do in return is get to know their names. Knowing what tree you are leaning against or standing under will give you an amazing insight into what's going on all around you. Being able to identify a tree means you can have a good guess at what species of butterfly and moth caterpillars may be chewing through its leaves, which birds may be nesting in its boughs and what fungi might burst through the leaf litter come the autumn.

But where to start? Well, you have already made the first step in tree identification – you're holding this book!

Inside, there are fifty fantastic tree species to discover, including those you may already recognise. On each page you will find a species clearly presented. Use the images of the leaf, twig and tree shape to help with identification. Find essential information in the factfile, and use the photofile to discover what wildlife you might see living in or near the tree. Take notes and record your sightings and activities with the stickers. If you find an ancient tree, don't forget to hug it and record your results at www.ancienttreehunt.org.uk

Enjoy learning about these fascinating and important plants, and start separating the wood from the trees, or should that be the trees from the wood?

Nick Baker

Seasonwatch

Each season brings with it different natural events and changes to wildlife, such as bluebells flowering in spring and blackberries ripening in summer. For fun things to do all year round visit naturedetectives.org.uk

SPRING

Trees that have been bare all winter come to life in spring. From late February to early March, leaf buds start to grow. With little else to eat, birds search for leftover seeds and insects on and around trees. By April, leaves are opening and flowers are blooming. By May, oaks, horse chestnuts and hawthorns are in full flower.

SUMMER

By June, many flowering trees are in full bloom. Butterflies, such as red admirals and peacocks, can be seen visiting flowers in hedgerows and woodland. Elder flowers bloom, producing a strong, sweet scent. Oaks are having a second growth spurt and new stems and leaves can be seen on the tips of their branches.

AUTUMN

As trees change in preparation for winter, their leaves turn a glorious array of browns, oranges and reds. Fruits ripen, attracting animals and birds. Once oak leaves have fallen, look for 'oak apples', or galls, on the tree. These are parts of the tree – buds, leaves or roots – that have swollen because insects have laid their eggs inside them.

WINTER

By winter, deciduous trees have lost their leaves. Squirrels and birds still visit them in search of fallen fruits, or to reach their nests. Small mammals, such as hedgehogs, often hibernate in the piles of leaves around a tree's base. At winter's end, male hazel catkins release clouds of yellow pollen to fertilise the small, red female flowers.

The Ancient Tree Hunt

The Ancient Tree Hunt is the Woodland Trust's project to find and map Britain's oldest trees. Join the hunt to discover these amazing trees, and use the pages in this book to record your findings. Find out more at www.ancienttreehunt.org.uk

What is an ancient tree?

An ancient tree is one that is very old and worth looking after for the future. Not all trees live to the same age – it depends on the type, or species, of tree. A willow tree that reaches 100 years of age would be in the last stages of its life, but a 100-year-old oak tree would still be a youngster!

ANCIENT TREES – Things to look for:

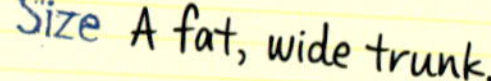

Size A fat, wide trunk.

Holes Large hollows in the trunk and deep cracks in the bark.

Fungus Mushrooms, toadstools and other fungi growing on the tree (this shows the heart of the tree is rotting and that it's very old).

Wow factor Ancient trees often look special. They have character and appear a bit battered and worn!

The Fortingall yew

The Fortingall yew in Scotland is thought to be about 5000 years old, and possibly the oldest-living thing in Europe. This tree has been a witness to history since Stone Age people lived in Scotland, through the Bronze Age, the Roman invasion, the Norman Conquest and the rise of modern Britain. It was already a few hundred years old when the ancient Egyptians began building the Pyramids at Giza!

Every tree in this book has an activity and each page tells you which one to do. For trees that can live to an ancient age, measure the girth of the trunk:

Measure the girth

YOU WILL NEED:

Pen/pencil

Friends

Measuring tape

Camera

If you have one, take a measuring tape, but if you don't, you can estimate the girth of the tree by hugging it!

1.5m

Measuring tape Measure around the trunk at 1.5 metres from the ground. If it you can't measure the tree at this height then make a note of the height at which you measured the girth.

Hugging A standard British hug (fingertip to fingertip) is 1.5 m long. With friends, wrap your arms around the trunk so that your fingertips touch each others' fingertips. Each person around the tree equals one 'hug'.

If you can, work out exactly where the tree is on a map. Take some photos of the tree, too, and upload them when you record your results at:

1.5 METRES: ONE BRITISH STANDARD HUG

www.ancienttreehunt.org.uk

HUGGED IT?

Once you have taken your measurements, remember to place your 'Hugged it!' sticker.

Many tree species are more short-lived. For these, try measuring the height:

Measure the height

YOU WILL NEED:

1 Ask a friend to stand next to the tree.

2 Facing the tree, hold your ruler upright and at arms length. Walk away from the tree until it 'fits' on the ruler.

3 According to the ruler, record how tall your friend is and how tall the tree is. Work out how many times your friend goes into the height of the tree.

4 Multiply this number by your friend's actual height (in metres) and this will give you the height of the tree.

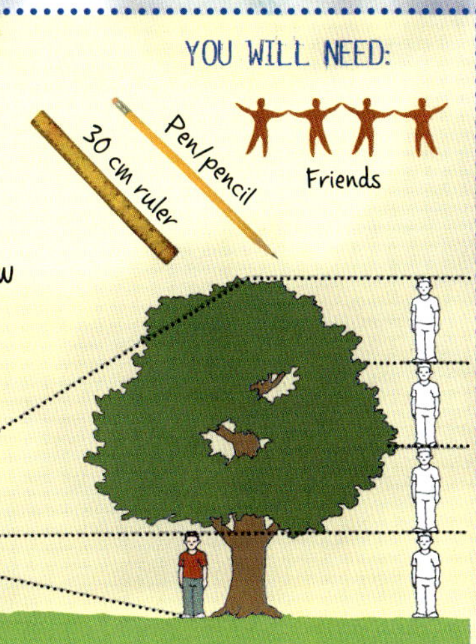

MEASURED IT?

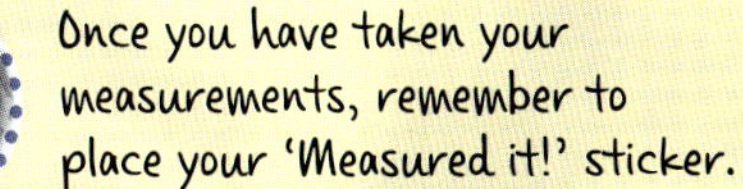

Once you have taken your measurements, remember to place your 'Measured it!' sticker.

How to plant a tree

Planting trees is great for the environment and easier than you might think. Choose a native tree and the benefits are even greater as these provide food and shelter for our wildlife.

Planting your tree from a seed

Try planting a tree from seeds you have collected yourself. You can collect seeds from late summer to autumn, once they have started dropping from trees.

Collecting and preparing

Cones Let cones dry out naturally and they will release their seeds.

Fleshy fruits Remove all flesh from seeds, such as cherries, berries and apples, and put in water. Only use the seeds that sink.

Nuts De-shell nuts, such as acorns and conkers, and put in water. Keep the nuts that sink.

Winged seeds Break in half to separate pairs. These can be planted with wings on.

Planting

1 All of the these seeds can be planted immediately in a container. Use small plant pots, old milk cartons or yogurt pots. Make holes in the bottom for drainage.

2 Fill containers with a mix of peat-free compost and sand. Sow alder, birch or pine seeds on top and cover with a thin layer of compost. Acorns and nuts should be sown about 5 cm deep. Press down the compost.

3 You can leave the pots outside over autumn and winter. Put them in a shady spot against a wall and cover with mesh to protect from birds and mice.

4 Once your seeds have germinated in spring, keep them watered well. When your seedlings are 20 to 40 cm tall they are ready to plant out.

TOP TREE-PLANTING TIPS

- If you have a small garden, avoid willow and poplar. Try hawthorn, hazel, holly, rowan, crab apple or box.
- If you have a large, spacious garden, try oak, ash, beech, Scots pine or yew.
- Make sure there is enough room for your tree to grow – don't plant it too close to buildings or pipes.
- If you are planting more than one tree, leave 2 metres between them.

Planting your tree from a sapling

An easy way to plant a tree is from a sapling (partly grown tree). You can buy saplings from your local garden centre, or online at www.nativetreeshop.com

1 Before planting your sapling, give the roots a good soak in a bucket of water.

2 Carefully remove the sapling from its container. Check it for damage and remove any broken roots.

3 Decide on your planting spot. Dig a hole twice as wide and slightly deeper than the roots. Save the turf for later.

4 You may need to make the hole bigger to avoid bending the roots – try your sapling in the hole to check.

5 Place your sapling upright in the hole. Break up the dug-out soil and fill in carefully but firmly around the roots.

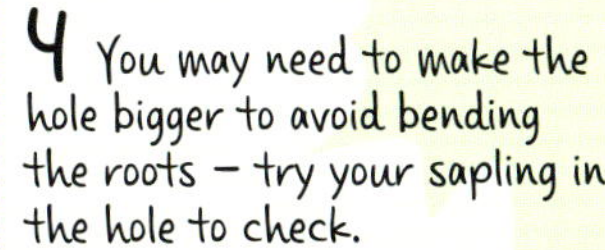

6 Tread down the soil firmly and add some more soil if needed. Tread down again.

7 Take the pieces of turf saved from earlier and place them upside down around your sapling and press them down.

8 Finally, 'heel in' the earth around the tree. Give your sapling a gentle tug – it should be firmly in place.

9 Tidy up and apply mulch (material laid down to keep in moisture) around the base of your sapling.

10 Start your tree diary.

LOOKING AFTER YOUR TREE

Now that you have planted your tree, you need to look after it:

- Keep a one-metre-circle around the base free from grass and plants for the first year.
- Add some mulch around the base. Bark mulch is best, but newspaper or grass clippings are better than nothing! Mulch provides nutrients to the tree and keeps in moisture.
- Check the tree regularly. 'Heel it in' (press firmly round the base with your heel) if it's rocked in the wind.
- Small trees planted in the winter shouldn't need watering, but larger trees may need watering through the first year and during dry spells.

For more information on planting trees, visit www.naturedetectives.org.uk

How to use this book

Use this guide to help you find your way around this book. Read information about 50 different species of trees, including vital statistics, wildlife you might see near the tree, detailed illustrations and simple identification tips.

Factfile
Provides vital statistics and information.

Nature detectives
Visit the nature detectives website for more information about trees and for lots of fun things to do all year round.

Photofile
If you spot the bug, bird or fungus featured for each tree, place a 'Seen it!' sticker.

My notes
Make notes about your tree sightings and stick in a leaf or photo of the tree on the right-hand side.

Activities
Complete the activity for each tree and place a 'Hugged it!' or 'Measured it!' sticker (see page 7).

www.naturedetectives.org.uk

FACTFILE

Height 20–25 m
Where Southern England, Ireland; often near water
Flowering March/April
Fruiting April/May
Leaf tint/fall October
Other names Water poplar
Uses Boat building, floorboards

PHOTOFILE

The striking hornet moth is rare in the UK. Adult moths lay their eggs in poplar trees, including black poplar. The larvae hatch and burrow into the wood, developing into adults in June and July.

MY NOTES

Season:

Where is the tree?

Describe the tree:

What wildlife can you see?

How many hugs is this tree?

HUGGED IT?

Record your hug results at www.ancienttreehunt.org.uk

STICK YOUR LEAF OR PHOTO HERE

On my tree I saw: leaves buds fruit flowers

18

Identifying a tree

1 Look at the leaf... What basic leaf shape do you think it is – oval, long, hand-shaped, compound or needle?

2 Go to that section of the book and see if you can find the same leaf.

3 Use the other illustrations to confirm your identification.

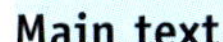

Main text
Every right-hand page has a main paragraph to introduce you to each species.

Rare in wild
Some trees are very rarely seen growing in the wild, so if you see one you're very lucky!

Scale guide

Each tree in this book is compared against a person silhouette. This will help you to understand how big or small it actually is.

An average person is about 1.8 m in height

Black poplar *Populus nigra*

RARE IN WILD

Once common along riverbanks, today the native black poplar is very rare and found only in southern England and parts of Ireland.

Black poplars are either male or female. Only a few hundred female trees exist in Britain and few of them grow near males. This means that seeds are rarely produced, so new trees are hard to find. Arrows found on the wreck of the *Mary Rose* were made of black poplar wood – they had survived 400 years beneath the sea.

DECIDUOUS

Smooth and tan coloured

Male catkins (flowers) are red

Up to 6 cm long

Green female catkins develop into seed capsules (fruit)

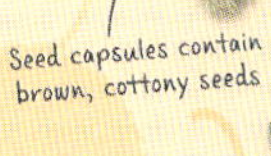

Can range from diamond to triangular in shape

Seed capsules contain brown, cottony seeds

Fine tooth on edge

OVAL

insects ○ birds ○ mammals ○ fungi ○ other . . . .

19

Tree shape
Refer to the tree shapes to help identify the tree at different times of the year.

Champion trees
This tells you the biggest known example of the species found in Britain, and you can find the champion trees featured in this book on the poster.

Leaf and twig
Use the leaf and twig to help identify the tree in summer or winter. (Evergreens do not have a winter twig because they don't lose their leaves).

Leaf shape
Use this icon to flick through the book to find the correct leaf shape section.

Tick list
Tick to record what you've seen on and around the tree.

Illustrations
These show what the fruits and flowers of each species look like.

FACTFILE

Height 18–25 m

Where Widespread; woodland, hedgerows, often near water

Flowering February/March

Fruiting October–December

Leaf tint/fall November

Other names Black alder, fearnog (Irish)

Uses Canal lock gates, charcoal

PHOTOFILE

The brown roll-rim fungus can be found from late summer to autumn growing at the foot of deciduous trees, including alder. This fungus often grows near edible mushrooms, but it is poisonous.

SEEN IT?

MY NOTES

Season:

Where is the tree?

Describe the tree:

What wildlife can you see?

How tall is your tree?

MEASURED IT?

On my tree I saw: leaves ○ buds ○ fruit ○ flowers ○

Alder *Alnus glutinosa*

The wood of the alder is fascinating – when it is submerged in water, it becomes as hard as stone.

Much of the Italian city of Venice is built on piles of alder wood, which were sunk into the sand banks. Houses and other buildings were then built on top. The small, winged seeds of this water-loving tree get carried along by streams and rivers to grow further downstream. It is said that the green dye of the alder flower was used to colour the clothes of Robin Hood.

DECIDUOUS

CHAMPION TREE
CHATSWORTH PARK,
DERBYSHIRE
GIRTH 609 cm

Rounded with toothed edges

Male catkins (flowers) are up to 5 cm long

Smaller female catkins develop into cones (fruit)

Mature cones are woody and open to release seeds

Shiny and dark green in colour

Side buds are on short stalks

OVAL

insects ○ birds ○ mammals ○ fungi ○ other . . . .

FACTFILE

Height 15–25 m

Where Widespread; hillsides, hedgerows, often near water

Flowering March

Fruiting May

Leaf tint/fall October

Other names Quaking aspen

Uses Matches, paper, boxes for fruit and vegetables

PHOTOFILE

Great spotted woodpeckers are common in woodlands. Their colours and patterns make them easy to spot. Their tapping on tree trunks, including those of aspen, can be heard particularly in early spring.

SEEN IT?

MY NOTES

Season:

Where is the tree?

Describe the tree:

What wildlife can you see?

How tall is your tree?

MEASURED IT?

STICK YOUR LEAF OR PHOTO HERE

On my tree I saw: leaves O buds O fruit O flowers O

Aspen *Populus tremula*

Fluttering leaves, which tremble in the breeze, give the aspen its Latin name *tremula* and its common name of 'quaking aspen'.

The autumn-dry leaves of the aspen produce a rustling noise even in gentle breezes. Herbalists once used its flowers to treat people suffering from anxiety or nightmares. In Medieval times, the timber was used to make houses for the poor who could not afford oak. Charcoal made from aspen wood was used in the production of gunpowder.

DECIDUOUS

Male and female catkins (flowers) grow on separate trees

Male catkins are reddish purple and up to 8 cm long

Buds have pointed tips

Rounded or slightly oval

Green female catkins develop into seed capsules (fruit) that contain many hairy seeds

Tiny, fluffy seeds are easily carried in the wind

In summer, new leaves emerge coppery brown, turning to green

OVAL

insects ○ birds ○ mammals ○ fungi ○ other . . . .

FACTFILE

Height 10–35 m

Where Southern and eastern England, South Wales; woodland, chalky or sandy soils

Flowering April/May

Fruiting September–November

Leaf tint/fall November–April

Other names Fea (Irish)

Uses Furniture, kitchen utensils

PHOTOFILE

Oyster fungi grow in forms called brackets on the trunks of beech and other deciduous trees. The topside is grey or cream, and it has white gills below. They are best seen in autumn.

SEEN IT?

MY NOTES

Season:

Where is the tree?

Describe the tree:

What wildlife can you see?

How many hugs is this tree?

HUGGED IT?

Record your hug results at www.ancienttreehunt.org.uk

On my tree I saw: leaves ○ buds ○ fruit ○ flowers ○

Beech *Fagus sylvatica*

Beech trees have long been part of Britain's history, especially in the furniture-making industry.

Particularly grand trees have been called 'queen beeches', and impressive beech woods are known as 'nature's cathedrals'. Since Roman times, beech wood was used for fuel and it was preferred for making furniture for its pink-orange colouring. Its nuts – called mast – were used as feed for animals.

DECIDUOUS

CHAMPION TREE
PLAS NEWYDD, ANGLESEY
GIRTH 962 cm

One or two nuts are held in a prickly four-lobed casing (fruit)

Triangular, shiny, brown nuts are called mast

Long, narrow buds

Pointed tip

Female flowers are green and spiky on short stems

Male flowers hang on long stems

Glossy and dark green

OVAL

insects 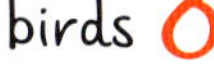 birds  mammals 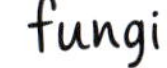 fungi  other . . . .

FACTFILE

Height 20–25 m

Where Southern England, Ireland; often near water

Flowering March/April

Fruiting April/May

Leaf tint/fall October

Other names Water poplar

Uses Boat building, floorboards

PHOTOFILE

The striking hornet moth is rare in the UK. Adult moths lay their eggs in poplar trees, including black poplar. The larvae hatch and burrow into the wood, developing into adults in June and July.

SEEN IT?

MY NOTES

Season:

Where is the tree?

Describe the tree:

What wildlife can you see?

How many hugs is this tree?

STICK YOUR LEAF OR PHOTO HERE

HUGGED IT?

Record your hug results at www.ancienttreehunt.org.uk

On my tree I saw: leaves ○ buds ○ fruit ○ flowers ○

Black poplar *Populus nigra*

Once common along riverbanks, today the native black poplar is very rare and found only in southern England and parts of Ireland.

Black poplars are either male or female. Only a few hundred female trees exist in Britain and few of them grow near males. This means that seeds are rarely produced, so new trees are hard to find. Arrows found on the wreck of the *Mary Rose* were made of black poplar wood – they had survived 400 years beneath the sea.

DECIDUOUS

Male catkins (flowers) are red

Up to 6 cm long

Smooth and tan coloured

Green female catkins develop into seed capsules (fruit)

Seed capsules contain brown, cottony seeds

Can range from diamond to triangular in shape

Fine tooth on edge

OVAL

insects  birds  mammals  fungi  other . . . .

FACTFILE

Height 6–7 m

Where Widespread; woodland, scrubland, hedgerows

Flowering March/April

Fruiting August/September

Leaf tint/fall October/November

Other names Sloe

Uses Walking sticks, fruits used in food and drink

PHOTOFILE

Dunnocks, also known as hedge sparrows, find shelter and berries to eat amongst blackthorn. Its branches grow tangled and spiny, making blackthorn a good tree for birds to build their nests.

SEEN IT?

MY NOTES

Season:

Where is the tree?

Describe the tree:

What wildlife can you see?

How tall is your tree?

MEASURED IT?

On my tree I saw: leaves ○ buds ○ fruit ○ flowers ○

Blackthorn *Prunus spinosa*

This deciduous tree is distinctive because its flowers are some of the first to appear in spring, appearing even before its leaves.

The fruits of the blackthorn are known as sloes and, although bitter to taste, they are popular with birds. It has long been considered a magical tree. In Celtic mythology it was home to fairies, and a blackthorn staff (long stick) was thought to be ideal for keeping evil spirits away.

Tiny, white, scented flowers have five petals and emerge before the leaves

Fruits are blue-black berries, called sloes

Dark, almost black in colour, and spiny

Sharply-pointed, stiff spines

Finely toothed edge

Dull green, 2 to 4 cm long

OVAL

insects ○ birds ○ mammals ○ fungi ○ other . . . .

FACTFILE

Height 6–8 m

Where Southern England; gardens, chalky soils

Flowering January–May

Fruiting August–September

Leaf tint/fall Evergreen

Other names Common box, boxwood

Uses Kitchen tools, engraving

PHOTOFILE

Box suckers are insects that spend winter as eggs on a box plant, hatching in spring. The larvae suck the tree's sap, making chemicals that stop the plant growing. Adults develop May to June.

SEEN IT?

MY NOTES

Season: ____

Where is the tree? ____

Describe the tree: ____

What wildlife can you see? ____

How tall is your tree? ____

MEASURED IT?

On my tree I saw: leaves ○ buds ○ fruit ○ flowers ○

Box *Buxus sempervirens*

RARE IN WILD

Slow-growing and never gaining great height, box is considered to be more of a shrub than a tree.

Its small, glossy, evergreen leaves grow tightly together, making it a perfect plant for garden hedges. Box can be cut and shaped into ornamental bushes in a practice known as topiary. It has an unpleasant smell, which caused Queen Anne (1665–1714) to have it removed from the gardens of Hampton Court Palace. Although common in gardens, box is rare in the wild.

EVERGREEN

Male and female flowers grow together in clusters

Male flowers are yellow, female flowers are greenish

1.5 to 3 cm long on hairy twigs

Small, tough and glossy

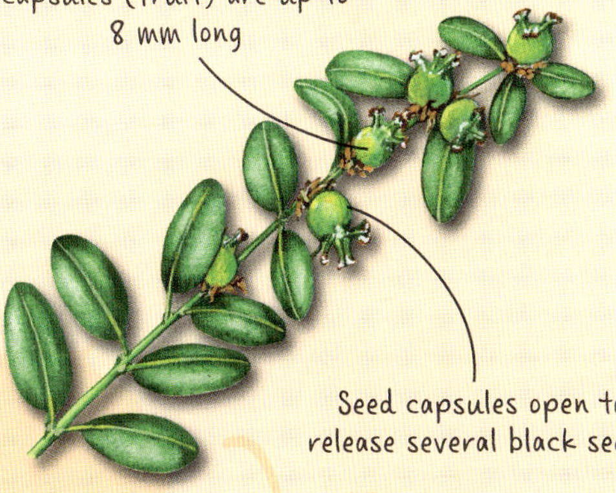

Three-horned, woody seed capsules (fruit) are up to 8 mm long

Seed capsules open to release several black seeds

OVAL

insects ○ birds ○ mammals ○ fungi ○ other ....

FACTFILE

Height 4–6 m

Where Widespread; hedgerows, woodland

Flowering May/June

Fruiting September/October

Leaf tint/fall October/November

Other names Common buckthorn, purging buckthorn

Uses Carving, kitchen utensils

PHOTOFILE

Brimstone butterflies lay their eggs on buckthorn leaves as this is the only plant eaten by the larvae. Adults hibernate over the winter and are one of the first butterflies to be seen in spring.

SEEN IT?

MY NOTES

Season:

Where is the tree?

Describe the tree:

What wildlife can you see?

How tall is your tree?

MEASURED IT?

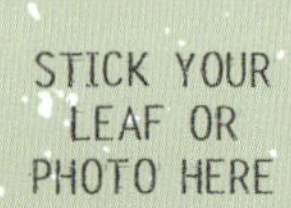

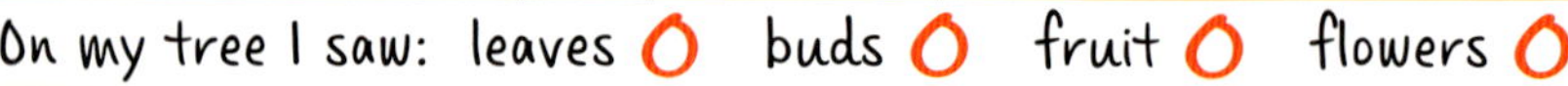

Buckthorn *Rhamnus cathartica*

In the past, plants and trees were used to treat illnesses and buckthorn is no exception.

The ripe, black berries are mildly poisonous to humans, but they are a good source of food for many birds. When herbal remedies were common, a tea made from buckthorn berries was used to treat a stomach ache, even though it causes vomiting and diarrhoea! Because of this, it is also referred to as purging buckthorn. The bark of a young tree is orange-brown and darkens with age.

DECIDUOUS

Flowers grow in clusters

Small, yellow, four-petalled flowers are scented

Sharp thorn at tip

Pointed tip

Fruits are berries that contain two to four seeds each

Shiny, black berries are up to 8 mm long

Dark and glossy with a smooth surface

OVAL

insects ◯ birds ◯ mammals ◯ fungi ◯ other . . . .

FACTFILE

Height 20–40 m

Where Widespread; woodland, parks, gardens, streets

Flowering July

Fruiting September

Leaf tint/fall October–November

Other names Common linden

Uses Carving, model building, guitar making

PHOTOFILE

The yellow-green lime aphid, *eucallipterus tiliae*, can be seen in spring and summer. Aphids are often regarded as pests because they feed on the tree's sap and can spread viruses.

SEEN IT?

MY NOTES

Season:

Where is the tree?

Describe the tree:

What wildlife can you see?

How many hugs is this tree?

HUGGED IT?

Record your hug results at www.ancienttreehunt.org.uk

On my tree I saw: leaves ○ buds ○ fruit ○ flowers ○

Common lime *Tilia x europaea (vulgaris)*

The widely planted common lime is easy to spot as its leaves, and anything under them, get covered in a sticky substance called honeydew.

Tiny insects called aphids suck sap (a sugary liquid) from the tree and produce honeydew. This attracts dirt, and by autumn, the leaves are sticky and filthy and so are cars that may be parked beneath its branches. Beekeepers often place their hives near lime trees so that the bees produce 'lime honey'.

DECIDUOUS

CHAMPION TREE
HOLKER HALL, CUMBRIA
GIRTH 789 cm

An extra leaflet, called a bract, helps the fruits to travel in the wind

Small, hard, round fruits

Red buds

5 to 10 cm long with a pointed tip

Groups of small, yellow, five-petalled flowers hang on long stalks

Scented

Look at the back of the leaf – if it has small clumps of red hairs at the base of the veins, it could be a small-leaved lime

Slightly heart-shaped with tufts of hair on the underside

OVAL

insects ○ birds ○ mammals ○ fungi ○ other . . . .

FACTFILE

Height 7–9 m

Where Widespread, except Scotland; woodland, hedgerows

Flowering April/May

Fruiting September/October

Leaf tint/fall October/November

Other names Wild crab

Uses Carving, mallets, tool handles, fruits made into jelly

PHOTOFILE

The autumn fruits of the crab apple tree attract greenfinches, along with many other birds. Greenfinches gather together in large flocks to feed, making lots of noise as they call to one another.

SEEN IT?

MY NOTES

Season: ____________________

Where is the tree?

____

____

____

Describe the tree:

____

____

____

____

What wildlife can you see?

____

____

____

How tall is your tree?

____

MEASURED IT?

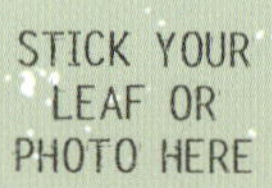

STICK YOUR LEAF OR PHOTO HERE

On my tree I saw: leaves ○ buds ○ fruit ○ flowers ○

Crab apple *Malus sylvestris*

Crab apples have been cultivated (grown especially) for hundreds of years, but a truly wild tree can be told apart by its thorns.

These trees produce small, sour apples that are not good to eat raw. However, they are often made into tasty crab apple jellies and jams. Crab apple wood is hard, heavy and strong, making it ideal for items that endure heavy wear, such as tools and handles. The wood produces a pleasant aroma (smell) when burnt.

DECIDUOUS

Reddish-brown with small buds (wild trees also have thorns)

Petals are white with pink tinges

Flowers are up to 4 cm across and grow in clusters

Toothed edges and a pointed tip

Young fruits are yellow-green, and rosy-red and green when ripe

Long stalk

The small apples grow up to 4 cm in diameter

OVAL

insects  birds mammals  fungi other . . . .

FACTFILE

Height 2–5 m

Where Widespread; woodland, scrubland, hedgerows

Flowering May/June

Fruiting September–November

Leaf tint/fall October/November

Other names Bloodtwig

Uses Skewers, arrow shafts, lamp oil can be made from fruits

PHOTOFILE

Robins often build their nests in hedgerows, including those of dogwood. Two broods of up to six blue eggs are laid from April to August. The berries also provide food for robins in autumn.

SEEN IT?

MY NOTES

Season: ____________________

Where is the tree? ____________________

____

____

____

Describe the tree: ____________________

____

____

____

____

What wildlife can you see? ____________________

____

____

____

How tall is your tree? ____________________

____

MEASURED IT?

STICK YOUR LEAF OR PHOTO HERE

On my tree I saw: leaves ○ buds ○ fruit ○ flowers ○

Dogwood *Cornus sanguinea*

This small tree or shrub has red-tinted stems that are especially noticeable in winter when there are few colours to brighten the dark days.

Dogwood has nothing to do with dogs. The wood is hard and was once used to make skewers known as 'dags'. This gave the tree its old name of dagswood. The leaves of dogwood can be identified by gently pulling them apart – a stringy latex can be seen where the veins have been broken.

DECIDUOUS

Small, white, bad-smelling flowers grow in clusters

Flowers have four petals and are up to 1 cm across

Reddish in colour

Smooth edges and deep veins with a pointed tip

Fruits are black, pea-sized berries

Berries are bitter to taste and not good to eat

Leaves turn dark red in autumn

OVAL

insects ◯ birds ◯ mammals ◯ fungi ◯ other . . . .

FACTFILE

Height 16–30 m

Where Widespread; woodland, hedgerows

Flowering February/March

Fruiting April–June

Leaf tint/fall October/November

Other names Field elm

Uses Before metal, the wood was used for water pipes

PHOTOFILE

Elm bark beetles can cause death to an elm. They spread Dutch elm disease – a fungus that infects the tree. The beetles chew holes into the wood to lay their eggs, and the larvae feed on wood.

SEEN IT?

MY NOTES

Season:

Where is the tree?

Describe the tree:

What wildlife can you see?

How many hugs is this tree?

HUGGED IT?

Record your hug results at www.ancienttreehunt.org.uk

On my tree I saw: leaves ○ buds ○ fruit ○ flowers ○

English elm *Ulmus procera*

English elms were common in Britain, until the onset of Dutch elm disease killed 25 million of them in the 1970s.

It is thought that this tree was introduced to Britain 2000 years ago by the Romans, and some scientific research suggests that all English elms descended from just one tree. This meant that many elms were equally vulnerable in the face of disease. Today, elms can often be seen growing in hedgerows.

Purple flowers are in small clusters

Flowers appear before the leaves

Thick and reddish colour

Toothed edges

Papery, winged fruits contain one seed each

Fruits are on short stalks

One side is longer than the other, similar to the wych elm

OVAL

insects ◯ birds ◯ mammals ◯ fungi ◯ other . . . .

FACTFILE

Height 4–10 m

Where Widespread; woodland, hedgerows

Flowering March/April

Fruiting May

Leaf tint/fall October/November

Other names Pussy willow, great sallow

Uses Stems used in basket making

PHOTOFILE

The red underwing moth, which is often seen on willows, is only found in southern, central and eastern England. The moth's forewings look like bark, helping it to stay safe from predators.

SEEN IT?

MY NOTES

Season:

Where is the tree?

Describe the tree:

What wildlife can you see?

How tall is your tree?

MEASURED IT?

On my tree I saw: leaves ○ buds ○ fruit ○ flowers ○

Goat willow *Salix caprea*

The goat willow is also known as 'pussy willow' because its springtime male catkins are soft and grey – like a cat's paw.

DECIDUOUS

Goat willows are important trees in woodland and hedgerows because they are closely associated with many types of butterfly and moth. Some larvae feed on the leaves and others live under the bark, feeding on the wood. As the male catkins mature and turn yellow they are called 'goslings' because they are the same colour as baby geese.

Grey at first, turning to yellow

Male catkins (flowers) are up to 10 cm long and silky to touch

Buds are green with a reddish tint

Male and female catkins appear on different trees

Long and oval

Female catkins (flowers) are green and longer than males

Upright seed capsules (fruit) hold lots of silky, hairy seeds

Dull green, and slightly hairy on upper surface

OVAL

insects ◯ birds ◯ mammals ◯ fungi ◯ other . . . .

FACTFILE

Height 12–15 m

Where Widespread; woodland, scrubland, hedgerows

Flowering February

Fruiting August/September

Leaf tint/fall November

Other names Coll (Irish)

Uses Walking sticks, stems used for fences and baskets

PHOTOFILE

Like many birds, jays survive the winter by storing food. They collect and hide hazelnuts and acorns amongst leaf litter and moss on the ground. They dig them up months later to eat.

SEEN IT?

MY NOTES

Season:

Where is the tree?

Describe the tree:

What wildlife can you see?

How many hugs is this tree?

STICK YOUR LEAF OR PHOTO HERE

HUGGED IT?

Record your hug results at www.ancienttreehunt.org.uk

On my tree I saw: leaves ○ buds ○ fruit ○ flowers ○

Hazel *Corylus avellana*

As hazel catkins turn yellow it's a sign that spring is coming, and when squirrels start to gather hazelnuts winter is just around the corner.

Hazels are not only a source of food for many types of wildlife, but they provide home and shelter for them too. They often grow in dense clusters with lots of stems growing from the ground, rather than a single trunk.

DECIDUOUS

Stiff hairs and small, oval buds

OVAL

insects ○ birds ○ mammals ○ fungi ○ other ....

FACTFILE

Height 10–20 m

Where Southern and eastern England; woodland, hedgerows

Flowering March

Fruiting September

Leaf tint/fall November–April

Other names Musclewood, ironwood

Uses Chopping blocks, charcoal

PHOTOFILE

Hawfinches can often be seen perching in the tops of trees, including hornbeam. These birds have large, powerful bills that they use to crack open the hornbeam's tough nuts.

SEEN IT?

MY NOTES

Season:

Where is the tree?

Describe the tree:

What wildlife can you see?

How many hugs is this tree?

HUGGED IT?

Record your hug results at www.ancienttreehunt.org.uk

On my tree I saw: leaves O buds O fruit O flowers 

Hornbeam *Carpinus betulus*

The statuesque hornbeam is an impressive deciduous tree with its pale silvery-grey bark, and yellow-green catkins in the spring.

It's often coppiced (stems cut back to the ground causing many long shoots to grow) or pollarded (top branches cut) and it is commonly planted for hedging. The white wood is very fine-grained, which makes particularly good firewood and charcoal. The Romans made their chariots from the wood because of its strength.

DECIDUOUS

CHAMPION TREE
HATFIELD FOREST, ESSEX
GIRTH 450 cm

Long buds

Pointed tip

Male catkins (flowers) are yellow-green with red specks

Green female catkins develop into fruits

Fruits are tough nuts with a three-lobed leaflet, or bract, attached

Double-toothed edge

OVAL

insects 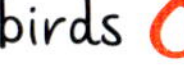 birds  mammals  fungi  other . . . .

FACTFILE

Height 8–10 m

Where England; mostly gardens

Flowering May

Fruiting July

Leaf tint/fall October/November

Other names Black mulberry, Persian mulberry, sycamine tree

Uses Fruits are eaten raw or made into jam

PHOTOFILE

The seven-spotted ladybird is the most common ladybird in Europe. From February, they can be seen on plants, and trees such as mulberrys. Ladybirds hibernate in groups during winter.

SEEN IT?

MY NOTES

Season:

Where is the tree?

Describe the tree:

What wildlife can you see?

How tall is your tree?

MEASURED IT?

STICK YOUR LEAF OR PHOTO HERE

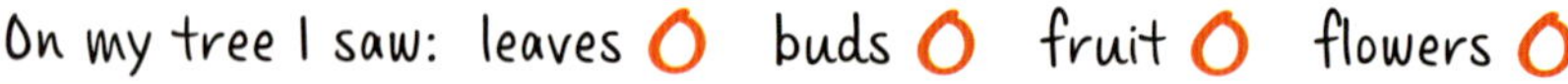

Mulberry *Morus nigra*

The black mulberry tree has a long history rooted in Southeast Asia where it has been cultivated for thousands of years.

It was introduced to Europe by the Romans, who dedicated the tree to Minerva, goddess of Wisdom. It has been widely planted and is grown in sheltered gardens for its delicious fruits, which contain a staining dye. It is celebrated in the nursery rhyme, 'Here we go round the mulberry bush'.

DECIDUOUS

Buds are broad and pointed

Male flowers are yellow-green and longer than the female flowers

Green female flowers are 1 to 2 cm long

Rough to touch on upper side

Raspberry-like fruits are purple-red when ripe

Fruits are sweet when ripe

Toothed edges

OVAL

insects  birds  mammals  fungi  other  ....

FACTFILE

Height 9–15 m

Where Southern England; orchards, woodland, gardens

Flowering March/April

Fruiting September/October

Leaf tint/fall November

Other names Common pear, European pear

Uses Wood is turned on a lathe to make bowls and similar objects

PHOTOFILE

Comma butterflies fly in late summer and early autumn and sometimes feed on fallen fruits, such as apples, pears and plums. The caterpillars feed on nettle, elm and hazel shoots.

SEEN IT?

MY NOTES

Season:

Where is the tree?

Describe the tree:

What wildlife can you see?

How tall is your tree?

MEASURED IT?

STICK YOUR LEAF OR PHOTO HERE

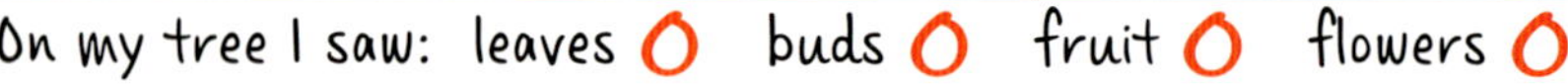

Pear *Pyrus communis*

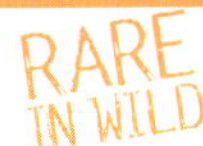

The pear tree originally came from Southwest Asia, but is now common throughout Europe.

Pears have undergone many changes since they first arrived in Europe as farmers have cultivated sweeter and juicier varieties of the fruit. Pear trees can be found in gardens and orchards in Britain, especially southern areas. The wild pear, which is a different type of pear, is rare, and its fruits are hard, gritty and smaller than those of the *Pyrus communis*.

DECIDUOUS

Flowers have five pure-white petals

Centres are pink-purple

Reddish-brown and hairy when young

Pointed tip

Fruits are hard pears up to 12 cm long

Pears ripen to yellow-green, sometimes slightly rosy

Smooth or finely toothed edge, up to 8 cm long

OVAL

insects 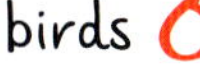 birds  mammals  fungi  other . . . .

FACTFILE

Height 8–10 m

Lifespan 20–40 years

Where Mainly England; orchards, gardens

Flowering April/May

Fruiting July–September

Leaf tint/fall October/November

Other names European plum

Uses Grown for fruit

PHOTOFILE

The larvae of the November moth feed on a wide range of trees, including plum and birch. Adult moths are hard to spot because their mottled grey-brown wings are perfectly camouflaged against bark.

SEEN IT?

MY NOTES

Season:

Where is the tree?

Describe the tree:

What wildlife can you see?

How tall is your tree?

MEASURED IT?

On my tree I saw: leaves ○ buds ○ fruit ○ flowers ○

Plum *Prunus domestica*

Plum trees are most commonly found growing in orchards and gardens.

Plums were probably created as a hybrid (mix) of blackthorn and cherry plum. Today, plums are the second-most cultivated fruit in the world. The plum *Prunus domestica* is first mentioned in 479 BC in the writings of the Chinese philosopher Confucius – it is listed as a popular food in Chinese culture. A tree will not produce fruit until it is four or five years old. Dried fruits are known as prunes.

DECIDUOUS

Smooth and brown

Smooth skin

Purple fruits are large, round and juicy

Clusters of flowers

Finely toothed edges

Flowers are all-white, sometimes tinged with green

Upper surface is smooth and lower surface has tiny hairs

OVAL

insects ○ birds  mammals  fungi ○ other . . . .

FACTFILE

Height 18–25 m

Where Widespread; woodland, scrubland

Flowering April–May

Fruiting June

Leaf tint/fall November

Other names Warty birch, beith (Irish)

Uses Cotton reels

PHOTOFILE

The birch polypore fungus grows on the trunks of birch trees in a shape called a bracket. Unlike photosynthesising plants, fungi take nourishment from the tree using tiny organs called 'hyphae'.

SEEN IT?

MY NOTES

Season: ________

Where is the tree? ________

Describe the tree: ________

What wildlife can you see? ________

How many hugs is this tree? ________

STICK YOUR LEAF OR PHOTO HERE

HUGGED IT?

Record your hug results at www.ancienttreehunt.org.uk

On my tree I saw: leaves ○ buds ○ fruit ○ flowers ○

Silver birch *Betula pendula*

With its silvery bark and fluttering leaves, the silver birch is sometimes called 'Queen of the forest'.

It was one of the first trees to start growing back in Britain at the end of the Ice Age, around 10,000 years ago. It is known as a pioneer species, which means it is one of the first plants to grow in a new area. Silver birch produces huge crops of seeds of up to one million every year. This tree is easily recognisable by its bark, even in the winter.

DECIDUOUS

CHAMPION TREE
PRIORY PARK, SURREY
GIRTH 399 cm

Winged seeds are 1 to 2 mm long and are released from the fruits

Brown, with small bumps, or warts

Slender, green female catkins (flowers) develop into seed capsules (fruit)

Double-toothed edges

Male catkins are long, drooping and yellow

Stalks are 1 to 2 cm long

OVAL

insects ○ birds ○ mammals ○ fungi ○ other . . . .

FACTFILE

Height Up to 6 m

Where South England, south Wales; hedgerows, scrubland, chalky soils

Flowering May

Fruiting August/September

Leaf tint/fall October/November

Other names Hoarwithy

Uses Young shoots can be made into twine

PHOTOFILE

The green hairstreak butterfly can often be seen on plants, such as the wayfaring tree, searching for flowers. Like many butterflies, the adults feed on nectar – a sweet liquid produced by flowers.

SEEN IT?

MY NOTES

Season: ____

Where is the tree? ____

Describe the tree: ____

What wildlife can you see? ____

How tall is your tree? ____

MEASURED IT?

STICK YOUR LEAF OR PHOTO HERE

On my tree I saw: leaves O buds O fruit O flowers O

Wayfaring tree *Viburnum lantana*

Once common alongside footpaths in southern England, the wayfaring tree grows in hedgerows, scrubland or on chalky ground.

Today, it is a more common sight in gardens, grown for its ornamental leaves, large flower heads and bright berries. Despite their attractive appearance, the berries are mildly poisonous and should not be eaten. The young and flexible stems can be used to make twine.

DECIDUOUS

White flowers appear in dense clusters

Flowers have five petals

Grey-brown and hairy

Underside is hairy

Fruits are oval berries that turn black when ripe

Berries are up to 8 mm long

Rough upper surface with deep veins

OVAL

insects 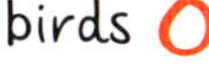 birds  mammals 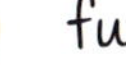 fungi 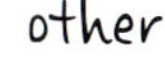 other . . . .

FACTFILE

Height 8–15 m

Where Southern England; woodland, chalky soils

Flowering May/June

Fruiting September

Leaf tint/fall October/November

Other names Common whitebeam

Uses Tool handles, furniture

PHOTOFILE

Whitebeam berries attract many birds, including waxwings, which are winter visitors to Britain. These unusually tame birds have crests on their heads and waxy red spots on their wings.

SEEN IT?

MY NOTES

Season:

Where is the tree?

Describe the tree:

What wildlife can you see?

How tall is your tree?

MEASURED IT?

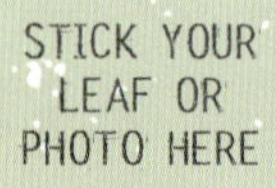

STICK YOUR LEAF OR PHOTO HERE

On my tree I saw: leaves ○ buds ○ fruit ○ flowers ○

Whitebeam *Sorbus aria*

When the leaves of the whitebeam first open in the spring they appear white, giving this tree its name ('beam' is the Saxon word for tree).

The whiteness is caused by the young leaves' soft coating of white hairs. Hair on the topside soon disappears as the leaves mature and droop downwards, but the undersides stay white. The wood of the whitebeam is very hard-wearing, and its small, red fruits can be made into jam and wine.

DECIDUOUS

White flowers grow in loose clusters

Green buds

Fruits are oval-shaped berries that turn red when ripe

Each berry contains two seeds

Up to 8 cm long

White hairs on the underside

OVAL

insects ○ birds ○ mammals ○ fungi ○ other . . . .

FACTFILE

Height 18–25 m

Where Widespread; parks, woodland

Flowering April/May

Fruiting July/August

Leaf tint/fall October/November

Other names Gean, crann silin (Irish)

Uses Furniture, veneers (thin layer of wood used in furniture making)

PHOTOFILE

Blackbirds are just one of many birds that flock around fruiting cherry trees to feed on their sweet fruits. Males are black with yellow beaks, and females are brown with spotted undersides.

SEEN IT?

MY NOTES

Season:

Where is the tree?

Describe the tree:

What wildlife can you see?

How tall is your tree?

MEASURED IT?

STICK YOUR LEAF OR PHOTO HERE

On my tree I saw: leaves ○ buds ○ fruit ○ flowers 

Wild cherry *Prunus avium*

When its branches are laden with white flowers or bunches of glossy fruits, the wild cherry attracts many birds.

According to folklore, this tree has particular associations with cuckoos. The birds are believed to need three good meals of cherries before they will stop singing. The wood of a cherry tree is fine-grained and a beautiful shade of red, making it popular with cabinet makers.

DECIDUOUS

CHAMPION TREE
STUDLEY ROYAL & FOUNTAINS ABBEY, YORKSHIRE
GIRTH 572 cm

Long, pointed tip

Brownish red buds

White, five-petalled flowers grow in groups of up to six

Berry-like fruits ripen to red

Up to 15 cm long with toothed edges

OVAL

insects  birds  mammals  fungi  other . . . .

FACTFILE

Height 3–5 m

Where Southern and central England, Wales; gardens, streets, parks

Flowering May/June

Fruiting September/October

Leaf tint/fall Semi-evergreen

Uses Planted for hedges

PHOTOFILE

The privet hawk moth lays its eggs on the leaves of privet, ash and lilac. When the larvae hatch, they feed on the leaves. Its wings and body have pink, white and brown markings.

SEEN IT?

MY NOTES

Season:

Where is the tree?

Describe the tree:

What wildlife can you see?

How tall is your tree?

MEASURED IT?

STICK YOUR LEAF OR PHOTO HERE

On my tree I saw: leaves ○ buds ○ fruit ○ flowers ○

Wild privet *Ligustrum vulgare*

For centuries, gardeners have taken wild trees and shrubs, such as privet, and grown them as ornamental plants.

Privet is one of few trees and shrubs that is described as being semi-evergreen. Depending on climate, sometimes it loses its leaves in winter and sometimes it doesn't. Privet is commonly grown in gardens and cut neatly into hedges, but the wild form looks very different, with long branches that reach upwards. The flowers and fruits were once used to treat eye and mouth diseases despite being poisonous.

Flowers grow in cone-shaped clusters

Cream-coloured, sweet-scented flowers attract insects

Small and shiny

Flowers develop into fruits

Fruits are shiny, black berries

Young twigs are covered in short hairs

OVAL

insects ○ birds ○ mammals ○ fungi ○ other ....

FACTFILE

Height 16–30 m

Where Widespread; hedgerows, woodland

Flowering February/March

Fruiting May/June

Leaf tint/fall October/November

Other names Scots elm

Uses Chests, water troughs, sea defences

PHOTOFILE

White-letter hairstreak butterflies only breed on elm. When these trees were struck down by disease in the 1970s, butterfly numbers dropped dramatically. The larvae of this butterfly are green.

SEEN IT?

MY NOTES

Season: ______

Where is the tree? ______

Describe the tree: ______

What wildlife can you see? ______

How many hugs is this tree? ______

STICK YOUR LEAF OR PHOTO HERE

HUGGED IT?

Record your hug results at www.ancienttreehunt.org.uk

On my tree I saw: leaves ○ buds ○ fruit ○ flowers ○

Wych elm *Ulmus glabra*

In Middle English (a language spoken long ago) the word 'wych' meant bendy.

Wych elm trees are not particularly bendy, but their young shoots are and they can be bent and twisted for making into baskets and other goods. These trees were badly affected by Dutch elm disease – a fungus carried by a wood-boring beetle. The leaves of the Wych elm are the largest of any native tree and can be up to 18 cm long!

DECIDUOUS

Flat, winged fruits are 2 cm long and contain one seed each

Purplish flowers grow in clusters

Covered in stiff hairs when young

Uneven base, similar to the English elm

Twelve to eighteen pairs of veins, more than the English elm

OVAL

insects ○ birds ○ mammals ○ fungi ○ other . . . .

FACTFILE

Height 8–15 m

Where Widespread; woodland, hedgerows, scrubland

Flowering April/May

Fruiting July

Leaf tint/fall Evergreen

Other names Holm, cuileann (Irish)

Uses Walking sticks, inlay work (in furniture making), engraving

PHOTOFILE

Holly blue butterflies lay two broods in the summer. The first brood is laid on holly and the second is laid on ivy. Both the carterpillars (larvae) and the adults feed on the leaves of both plants.

SEEN IT?

MY NOTES

Season:

Where is the tree?

Describe the tree:

What wildlife can you see?

How many hugs is this tree?

STICK YOUR LEAF OR PHOTO HERE

HUGGED IT?

Record your hug results at www.ancienttreehunt.org.uk

On my tree I saw: leaves ○ buds ○ fruit ○ flowers ○

Holly *Ilix aquifolium*

With its clusters of bright-red berries and prickly leaves, the holly tree is steeped in myth and mystery and is the subject of many superstitions.

Although it was thought that cutting holly would bring bad luck, the custom of bringing holly into the home at midwinter goes back thousands of years. Hanging holly was thought to ward off evil spirits, and with its evergreen leaves, this tree was thought to symbolise fertility and be an effective charm against witches and goblins.

insects ◯ birds ◯ mammals ◯ fungi ◯ other . . . .

FACTFILE

Height 12–25 m

Where Widespread; gardens, parks, arboretums

Flowering June–August

Fruiting September–December

Leaf tint/fall Evergreen

Other names Southern evergreen magnolia, bull bay

Uses Veneers, vegetable crates

PHOTOFILE

Wild rabbits are grey-brown in colour and are very common in the British countryside. In winter, when there is less food, they sometimes gnaw the bark of trees, including magnolia.

SEEN IT?

MY NOTES

Season:

Where is the tree?

Describe the tree:

What wildlife can you see?

How tall is your tree?

MEASURED IT?

STICK YOUR LEAF OR PHOTO HERE

On my tree I saw: leaves ○ buds ○ fruit ○ flowers ○

Magnolia *Magnolia grandiflora*

With their enormous, fragrant blooms and clusters of red seeds, magnolias are impressive trees that brighten up a garden.

They originally came from the United States and are the state flowers of Mississippi and Louisiana. Magnolias are normally fertilised by beetles. Its petals are unusually tough, which minimises damage by the crawling insects. They are named after Pierre Magnol (1638–1715), a French botanist, and many different varieties have been cultivated.

EVERGREEN

Six to twelve petals

Large, white, scented flowers up to 25 cm across

Furry seed capsules (fruit) are up to 6 cm long and turn from green to orange-pink

Thick and glossy with smooth edges

Seed capsules open to release red seeds

Up to 16 cm long

LONG

insects 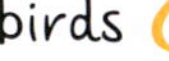 birds  mammals  fungi other . . . .

FACTFILE

Height 15–25 m

Where Widespread; ancient woodland

Flowering May

Fruiting October

Leaf tint/fall November

Other names Common oak, dair (Irish), English oak

Uses Building, furniture, floorboards

PHOTOFILE

The gall wasp lays its eggs inside the oak tree. As a larva grows, a protective growth forms around it called a gall, or 'oak apple'. The larva stays inside the gall until it has developed into an adult.

SEEN IT?

MY NOTES

Season:

Where is the tree?

Describe the tree:

What wildlife can you see?

How many hugs is this tree?

STICK YOUR LEAF OR PHOTO HERE

HUGGED IT?

Record your hug results at www.ancienttreehunt.org.uk

On my tree I saw: leaves ○ buds ○ fruit ○ flowers ○

Pedunculate oak *Quercus robur*

The pedunculate, or English, oak is known as the 'King of the forest' and it has a rich history, featuring in many myths and legends.

English oaks provide a unique habitat for hundreds of species of other plants and animals. Oaks attract insects, which in turn attract birds, and acorns provide food for squirrels and other small mammals. A single tree can live for hundreds of years.

DECIDUOUS

CHAMPION TREE
BOWTHORPE PARK FARM,
LINCOLNSHIRE
GIRTH 1279 cm

Cluster of buds at the tip

Male catkins (flowers) are green-yellow

Three to six rounded lobes on each side

Up to 3 cm long

Acorns (fruit) sit in cups at the end of long stalks, unlike the acorns of the sessile oak, which don't have stalks

Almost no stalk

LONG

insects ○ birds ○ mammals ○ fungi ○ other . . . .

FACTFILE

Height 1–3 m

Where Widespread; coastal areas, sand dunes

Flowering March/April

Fruiting September

Leaf tint/fall November

Uses Skewers, fruits used in herbal medicines and cosmetics

PHOTOFILE

Fieldfares visit Britain in winter searching for food, and the berries from sea buckthorn are a good source. White flashes under their wings help identify these birds, which are a type of thrush.

SEEN IT?

MY NOTES

Season:

Where is the tree?

Describe the tree:

What wildlife can you see?

How tall is your tree?

MEASURED IT?

STICK YOUR LEAF OR PHOTO HERE

On my tree I saw: leaves ○ buds ○ fruit ○ flowers ○

Sea buckthorn *Hippophae rhamnoides*

This small deciduous shrub can be found growing on exposed, windy coastlines in salty conditions that few other trees can tolerate.

Sea buckthorn is an increasingly popular plant that is cultivated for the extraordinary properties of its bright-orange berries and its deep and widespread roots. The berries are full of vitamin C and are used in skincare products. Its roots help to bind loose soil and add nitrogen to it, which is important for soil fertility.

insects ○ birds ○ mammals ○ fungi ○ other . . . .

FACTFILE

Height 15–30 m

Where Widespread; hillsides, woodland

Flowering April/May

Fruiting October/November

Leaf tint/fall November/ December

Other names Durmast oak, dair (Irish), darachor (Gaelic)

Uses Building, poles, fences

PHOTOFILE

Small, green oak bush crickets are often seen in the leaves of oak trees, but they also live around other deciduous trees. They are most active after dark and are common from July to late autumn.

SEEN IT?

MY NOTES

Season: ____

Where is the tree? ____

Describe the tree: ____

What wildlife can you see? ____

How many hugs is this tree? ____

STICK YOUR LEAF OR PHOTO HERE

HUGGED IT?

Record your hug results at www.ancienttreehunt.org.uk

On my tree I saw: leaves ○ buds ○ fruit ○ flowers ○

Sessile oak *Quercus petraea*

The sessile oak is one of just two native British oaks, but there are hundreds of different types in the northern hemisphere alone.

The sessile oak is more likely to be found in stony uplands than the pedunculate oak, but they are similar in appearance. In Anglo-Saxon times, an oak was called an 'aik' and a seed was an 'aik-com', hence today's name – acorn. In one year, a mature oak tree may produce as many as 50,000 acorns.

DECIDUOUS

CHAMPION TREE
COWDRAY PARK, WEST SUSSEX
GIRTH 1253 cm

Hard-shelled acorns (fruit) grow in clusters

Orange-brown buds

Sessile acorns do not have stalks, unlike pedunculate acorns which have long stalks

Paler underneath with hairs on veins

Male catkins are yellow and drooping

Leaf stalks are 1 to 2 cm – much longer than those of the pedunculate oak

LONG

insects 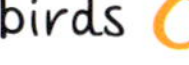 birds  mammals  fungi ○ other . . . .

FACTFILE

Height Up to 5 m

Where England, Wales; hedgerows, woodland

Flowering May/June

Fruiting September/October

Leaf tint/fall October/November

Other names Fusanum, fusoria, prickwood, skewerwood

Uses Skewers, spindles, knitting needles

PHOTOFILE

Also known as the hawthorn fly, the St Mark's fly lives around meadows and hedgerows on shrubs, including spindle. The female adults begin hatching around April 25th, which is St Mark's Day.

SEEN IT?

MY NOTES

Season: ______

Where is the tree? ______

Describe the tree: ______

What wildlife can you see? ______

How tall is your tree? ______

MEASURED IT?

STICK YOUR LEAF OR PHOTO HERE

On my tree I saw: leaves ○ buds ○ fruit ○ flowers ○

Spindle *Euonymus europaeus*

RARE IN WILD

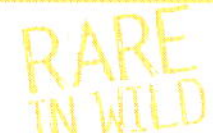

Spindles more often resemble bushes than trees, and they are often seen in hedgerows and woodlands.

The timber of this plant was once used to make spindles – round, spinning pieces of wood that wool is wound onto. This gave the spindle tree its common name. The poisonous berries contain orange seeds that can be boiled to make a yellow dye. The berries have also been used in traditional remedies to cure farm animals of skin complaints.

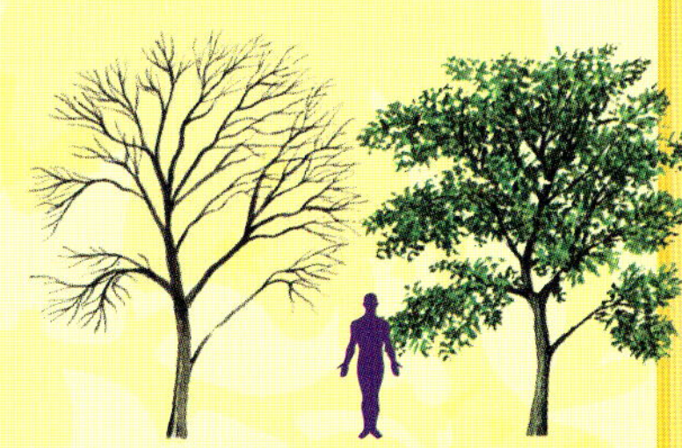

DECIDUOUS

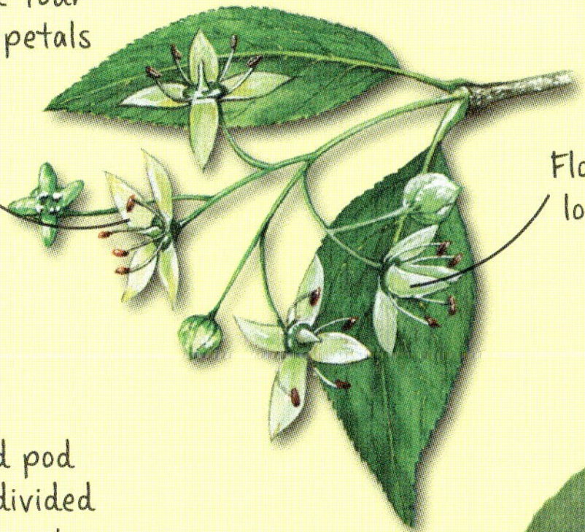

Flowers have four green-white petals
Flowers grow in loose clusters

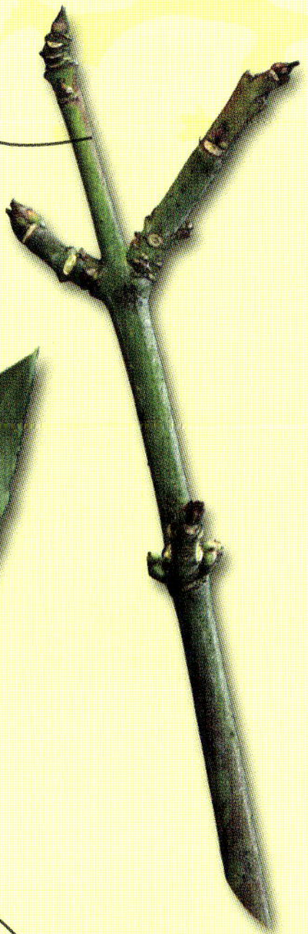

Green with shoots coming off at many angles

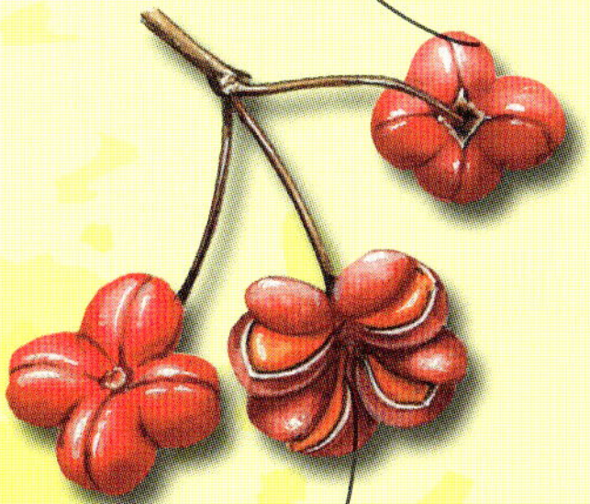

Each seed pod (fruit) is divided into four parts
Scarlet seed pods open to release four small, orange seeds

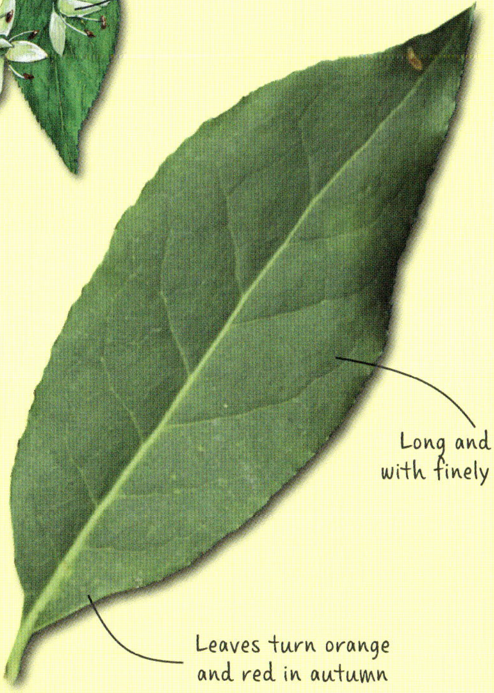

Long and oval-shaped with finely toothed edges
Leaves turn orange and red in autumn

LONG

insects ○ birds ○ mammals ○ fungi ○ other . . . .

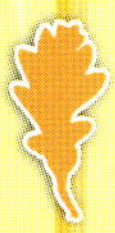

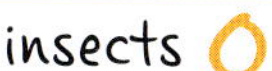

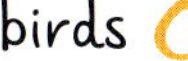

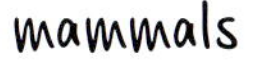

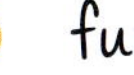

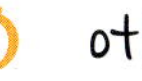

FACTFILE

Height 20–30 m

Where Widespread; woodland, parks, well-drained soil

Flowering June/July

Fruiting October/November

Leaf tint/fall October–December

Other names Spanish chestnut

Uses Stems used for fence poles, nuts roasted for eating

PHOTOFILE

Today, grey squirrels are common in the UK, since being introduced in the early 1900s. Their fur is grey, sometimes with brown tinges. Nutritious sweet chestnuts are one source of food for grey squirrels.

SEEN IT?

MY NOTES

Season: Summer 10/06/12

Where is the tree? CHRISTCHURCH C&C CLUB SITE FOREST OF DEAN

TREE BEARS 195°M 17M FROM

GPS BNG SO 56962 12762 POSITION

Describe the tree: IN FULL LEAF. TWIGS HAVE

WHITE DOTS. LEAF 17CM LONG

What wildlife can you see?

How many hugs is this tree? 2

305CM.

HUGGED IT!

Record your hug results at www.ancienttreehunt.org.uk

On my tree I saw: leaves ✓ buds fruit flowers 

Sweet chestnut *Castanea sativa*

These trees produce large, edible nuts that can be roasted and are often sold in streets, at fairs and other winter events.

Sweet chestnuts have been long associated with winter festivals and were once seen as sources of magic. They are native to the warmer parts of Europe and were first brought to Britain by Roman soldiers, who relied on the nuts as an important part of their diet. Sweet chestnuts do not always ripen fully in Britain.

DECIDUOUS

CHAMPION TREE
CANFORD SCHOOL, DORSET
GIRTH 1344 cm

Tiny white dots, or warts, along twig

Fruits open to reveal one to three glossy, brown nuts

Spiky, green casing

Long, male catkins (flowers) can grow as long as the leaves

10 to 25 cm long

Sharply toothed edges

Green, spiky female flowers grow at the base of the catkin

LONG

insects ○ birds ○ mammals ○ fungi ○ other . . . .

FACTFILE

Height 20–25 m

Where Widespread; often near water

Flowering April/May

Fruiting June–August

Leaf tint/fall October/November

Other names European willow, sailach (Irish)

Uses Medicine made from bark and leaves is similar to aspirin

PHOTOFILE

The beautiful song of a willow warbler marks the beginning of spring. These pretty birds visit Britain from April to October, and often perch in willow and birch trees looking for insects.

SEEN IT?

MY NOTES

Season: ________

Where is the tree? ________

Describe the tree: ________

What wildlife can you see? ________

How tall is your tree? ________

MEASURED IT?

STICK YOUR LEAF OR PHOTO HERE

On my tree I saw: leaves ○ buds ○ fruit ○ flowers ○

White willow *Salix alba*

The white willow grows well in damp soil and so is most likely to be found alongside streams and ponds, often near alder trees.

Animals, especially horses, enjoy nibbling the leaves and tender shoots of this tree. The pale brown wood of the white willow burns easily and quickly. This tree can be pollarded every four or five years to produce a crop of straight poles, which are used for making fences.

DECIDUOUS

Female catkins (flowers) are green and appear on separate trees to the males

Male catkins are yellow

Golden yellow with fine hairs

Finely toothed edges

Female catkins develop into seed capsules, full of hairy seeds

Long and narrow

Grey to pale brown in colour

LONG

insects  birds mammals 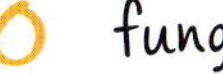 fungi  other . . . .

FACTFILE

Height 8–14 m

Where Widespread; woodland, hedgerows

Flowering April

Fruiting June/July

Leaf tint/fall November

Other names Hedge maple, English maple

Uses Wood used in violin making

PHOTOFILE

Sycamore moths have a wingspan of up to 4.5 cm. They are pale to dark grey in colour, and have a mottled pattern that helps to camouflage them. They feed on sycamores, maples and horse chestnuts.

SEEN IT?

MY NOTES

Season: ______

Where is the tree? ______

Describe the tree: ______

What wildlife can you see? ______

How many hugs is this tree? ______

HUGGED IT?

Record your hug results at www.ancienttreehunt.org.uk

On my tree I saw: leaves ○ buds ○ fruit ○ flowers 

Field maple *Acer campestre*

The field maple provides an ideal habitat for many small creatures, and plants such as lichens and mosses.

Field maples are often found growing in hedgerows. In autumn, they can be identified by their leaves, which turn red and yellow. According to ancient myths, a child could be guaranteed a long life by being passed through the branches of a field maple. In some places, it was thought that field maples could protect a house against bats.

DECIDUOUS

CHAMPION TREE
DOWNHAM CHURCHYARD.
ESSEX
GIRTH 452 cm

Brown and coated in soft hairs

Three to five rounded lobes

White-green flowers have five petals

Paired, winged fruits are like helicopter blades

4 to 7 cm long, smaller than a sycamore

The wings are in a straight line, not curved as in the sycamore

HAND-SHAPED

insects O birds O mammals O fungi O other ....

FACTFILE

Height Up to 4 m

Where Widespread; woodland, scrubland, hedgerows, damp soils

Flowering June/July

Fruiting September

Leaf tint/fall October/November

Other names Snowball bush

Uses Skewers

PHOTOFILE

Bullfinches are shy birds that can be difficult to spot. They hide in thickets and hedges, such as guelder rose, but their low, clear whistle may give them away. They eat buds, berries and seeds.

SEEN IT?

MY NOTES

Season:

Where is the tree?

Describe the tree:

What wildlife can you see?

How tall is you tree?

MEASURED IT?

STICK YOUR LEAF OR PHOTO HERE

On my tree I saw: leaves ○ buds ○ fruit ○ flowers ○

Guelder rose *Viburnum opulus*

Despite its name, this shrub is not a rose at all, but more closely related to the elder.

Its unusual name comes from the Dutch province of Guelderland where it was grown as a decorative garden plant. Guelder rose berries are popular with birds, such as bullfinches, and small animals, but they are poisonous to humans. The berries can be used to make a red ink.

DECIDUOUS

Clusters of small, white flowers are encircled by larger white flowers

Scented flowers have five petals

Buds grow in opposite pairs

8 cm long with three large lobes

Central flowers develop into red berries (fruit)

Leaves turn reddish-brown in autumn

Poisonous berries contain one seed each

HAND-SHAPED

insects ○ birds ○ mammals ○ fungi ○ other . . . .

FACTFILE

Height 12–15 m

Where Widespread; hedgerows, scrubland

Flowering May/June

Fruiting March/April

Leaf tint/fall November

Other names May, whitethorn, quickthorn, tramp's supper, holy innocents

Uses Walking sticks, tool handles

PHOTOFILE

The hawthorn shield bug has brown markings on its broad, shield-shaped back. It's common on hawthorn leaves, but also feeds on other types of shrub and tree, including oaks and whitebeam.

SEEN IT?

MY NOTES

Season:

Where is the tree?

Describe the tree:

What wildlife can you see?

How many hugs is this tree?

STICK YOUR LEAF OR PHOTO HERE

HUGGED IT?

Record your hug results at www.ancienttreehunt.org.uk

Hawthorn *Crataegus monogyna*

The hawthorn's frothy white blossom is a sign that summer is on its way.

Hawthorn is a popular hedgerow plant and its leaves are quick to appear in spring. In folklore, in North Wales, hawthorn was associated with death, possibly because the flowers' scent reminds some people of rotting flesh. However the berries, leaves and flowers have been used in many past medicines. It also has long associations with May Day – its wood was used to make the first Maypoles.

DECIDUOUS

CHAMPION TREE
HETHEL, NORFOLK
GIRTH 245 cm

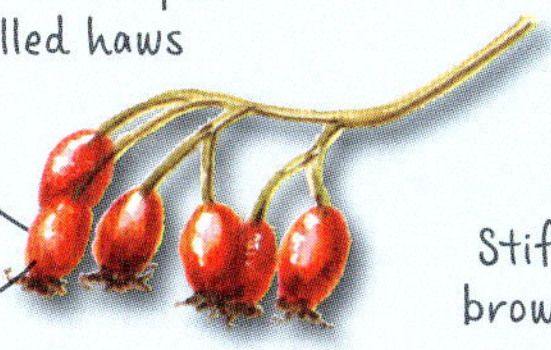

Deep red, oval-shaped fruits called haws

Stiff with brown buds

Haws contain one seed each, unlike those of the Midland hawthorn, which contain two

Long thorns up to 1.5 cm long

Dark green

Three to seven deep lobes

HAND-SHAPED

Small, white, scented flowers grow in clusters after the leaves have appeared

insects ○ birds ○ mammals ○ fungi ○ other . . . .

FACTFILE

Height 14–28 m

Where Widespread; woodland, parks, hedgerows

Flowering May

Fruiting September/October

Leaf tint/fall October/November

Other names Conker tree

Uses Extract from nuts is used to make herbal medicines

PHOTOFILE

Honey bees visit flowers, such as those of horse chestnut, for nectar. They also carry pollen on their bodies to other flowers. This helps fertilise the flowers so that they will produce seeds.

SEEN IT?

MY NOTES

Season:

Where is the tree?

Describe the tree:

What wildlife can you see?

How many hugs is this tree?

STICK YOUR LEAF OR PHOTO HERE

HUGGED IT?

Record your hug results at www.ancienttreehunt.org.uk

On my tree I saw: leaves ○ buds ○ fruit ○ flowers ○

Horse chestnut *Aesculus hippocastanum*

Horse chestnuts are best known for their glossy, brown nuts known as conkers.

Competitors meet up in Northamptonshire every year to battle in the World Conker Championships – an event that has been running since 1965. Horse chestnut trees arrived in Britain in the 16th century and possibly get their name from the practice of feeding conkers to horses to cure them of illness.

DECIDUOUS

Upright spikes of white flowers

Flowers have five petals and a small pink spot near the centre

Sticky buds

Leaves are made up of five to seven long leaflets and appear in early spring

One brown nut, or conker, inside each spiky, green fruit

About 6 cm wide

Leaflets fan out and are on a sturdy stalk

HAND-SHAPED

insects  birds mammals 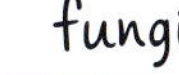 fungi other . . . .

FACTFILE

Height 13–35 m

Where Widespread; streets, parks, cities, towns

Flowering May/June

Fruiting September/October

Leaf tint/fall October/November

Other names Hybrid plane

Uses Furniture

PHOTOFILE

House sparrows used to be more common in towns and cities, perching in trees such as London planes. In recent years, their numbers have dropped. They feed on insects, seeds, berries and buds.

SEEN IT?

MY NOTES

Season: ______

Where is the tree? ______

Describe the tree: ______

What wildlife can you see? ______

How many hugs is this tree? ______

STICK YOUR LEAF OR PHOTO HERE

HUGGED IT?

Record your hug results at www.ancienttreehunt.org.uk

On my tree I saw: leaves ○ buds ○ fruit ○ flowers 

London plane *Platanus x hispanica*

London plane trees are a familiar sight in many cities and towns.

They were widely planted along streets in urban areas because they tolerate pollution. In the 17th century, American plane and oriental plane trees were cross-bred to produce this new variety. The London plane sheds dirt in it's bark, which peels off through the year revealing a paler yellow bark beneath. Its attractive, hard-wearing timber is also known as 'lacewood'.

DECIDUOUS

Male flowers are round and yellow

Female flowers are round and reddish

Green with smooth, pink buds

Lobes have triangular tips

Each spiky fruit contains many seeds

Many fruit cases stay on the tree throughout the winter

Up to 25 cm long

HAND-SHAPED

insects  birds mammals  fungi  other . . . .

FACTFILE

Height 16–35 m

Where Widespread; woodland, hedgerows, mountains

Flowering April/May

Fruiting September

Leaf tint/fall October/November

Other names Great maple, great plane, martyrs' tree

Uses Furniture, veneers, musical instruments

PHOTOFILE

In winter, the large, oval outline of a tawny owl may be seen against the branches of a sycamore tree. Owls prey on animals at night and have superb senses of eyesight and hearing.

SEEN IT?

MY NOTES

Season:

Where is the tree?

Describe the tree:

What wildlife can you see?

How many hugs is this tree?

HUGGED IT?

Record your hug results at www.ancienttreehunt.org.uk

On my tree I saw: leaves ○ buds ○ fruit ○ flowers 

Sycamore *Acer pseudoplatanus*

In the autumn, sycamores produce thousands of spinning, winged fruits called 'keys'.

The wings act like helicopter blades and spin the keys through the air so that they land a distance from the tree. The sycamore is also known as the martyrs' tree. In England in 1834, a group of workers – the Tolpuddle Martyrs – met under a sycamore to form a society to fight for better wages. They were expelled from the country as punishment.

DECIDUOUS

CHAMPION TREE
BIRNAM, PERTH & KINROSS
GIRTH 723 cm

Winged fruits, or keys, are green at first, then ripen to brown

Each key holds two seeds

Green buds grow in opposite pairs

Yellow-green flowers hang in spikes

Each individual flower has five petals

Stalks are often red

Up to 15 cm long with five lobes

HAND-SHAPED

insects ○ birds ○ mammals ○ fungi ○ other . . . .

FACTFILE

Height 10–25 m

Where Southern England, Wales; ancient woodland

Flowering May/June

Fruiting September–November

Leaf tint/fall October/November

Other names Chequers

Uses Fruits used to make an alcoholic drink called 'chequers'

PHOTOFILE

Redwings may be seen flying in flocks in autumn. These birds are a type of thrush and they eat insects, as well as berries from trees, such as rowan, hawthorn and the wild service tree.

SEEN IT?

MY NOTES

Season:

Where is the tree?

Describe the tree:

What wildlife can you see?

How tall is this tree?

MEASURED IT?

On my tree I saw: leaves ○ buds ○ fruit ○ flowers 

Wild service tree *Sorbus torminalis* RARE IN WILD

The wild service tree is an indicator of ancient woodland – areas where there has been continuous woodland since at least 1600.

In spring, white blossom covers this tree and in autumn, its leaves turn coppery-red. Its berries, which were used to cure stomach upsets until the 1700s, are best eaten when overripe. This tree also goes by the name of 'chequers'. Some say this refers to the bark peeling off in squares and leaving a chequerboard effect.

DECIDUOUS

Green buds

Stalks are hairy

Small white flowers hang in clusters on stalks

Reddish-brown, berry-like fruits

Up to 10 cm long

Slightly glossy on upper surface

HAND-SHAPED

insects ○ birds ○ mammals ○ fungi ○ other . . . .

FACTFILE

Height 15–30 m

Where Widespread; woodland, hedgerows, hillsides

Flowering April

Fruiting June

Leaf tint/fall September/October

Other names Lofty ash, fuinnseog (Irish)

Uses Oars, farm tools, spade handles

PHOTOFILE

King Alfred's cake fungus is also called coal fungus. It is ball-shaped and dark in colour. It grows on fallen trees, especially ash and beech. Dried fungus makes good tinder for fires.

SEEN IT?

MY NOTES

Season: Spring - 23/4/13

Describe the tree:

Three ash trees beside a stream, tall, bent, fairly slim. No leaves yet. Identified by flower clusters

Where is the tree?

(Caravan Club site)
At Weston Farm, C.C. Club side Weston-on-Avon, Warwicks

What wildlife can you see?

None. Birdsong heard. Sounds like 'pee-wit' at times.

How many hugs is this tree?

STICK YOUR LEAF OR PHOTO HERE

HUGGED IT?

Record your hug results at www.ancienttreehunt.org.uk

On my tree I saw: leaves ○ buds ○ fruit ○ flowers ○

Ash *Fraxinus excelsior*

The stately ash is one of the tallest deciduous trees in Europe and it grows easily in many habitats across Britain.

In Scandinavian mythology, the ash was regarded as the tree of life. In English folklore, it was used to predict the weather. If oak buds opened before ash buds then the summer would be dry, but if ash buds opened first, the summer would be wet. Like many trees, the ash was once believed to provide defence against black magic and witchcraft.

DECIDUOUS

CHAMPION TREE
MOCCAS PARK,
HEREFORDSHIRE
GIRTH 825 cm

Purplish clusters of petalless flowers

Black buds

Flowers appear before leaves

Three to six pairs of leaflets with a single leaflet at the tip

Winged fruits, called ash keys, hang in clusters

Toothed edges

Some keys stay on the tree through winter, after the leaves have fallen

COMPOUND

insects ○ birds ○ mammals ○ fungi ○ other . . . .

FACTFILE

Height Up to 10 m

Where Widespread; hedgerows, scrubland

Flowering June/July

Fruiting August/September

Leaf tint/fall October/November

Other names Elderflower, common elder, black elder

Uses Toys, wooden spoons

PHOTOFILE

Jelly ear fungus is a rubbery, ear-shaped fungus that is dark in colour. It often grows on dead elder and elm trees and is best seen in winter and spring. Each lobe can grow up to 10 cm across.

SEEN IT?

MY NOTES

Season: ______

Describe the tree: ______

Where is the tree? ______

What wildlife can you see? ______

How tall is your tree? ______

MEASURED IT?

On my tree I saw: leaves ○ buds ○ fruit ○ flowers ○

Elder *Sambucus nigra*

The elder has proved to be a useful British tree, with the flowers, berries and stems all being put to good use.

'Elder' comes from the Anglo Saxon word *aeld* meaning 'fire'. The stems are hollow and were once used to blow air into fires. In Denmark, the tree was associated with magic and, before a tree could be cut down, permission had to be sought from its spirit. The flowers can be made into a cordial and the berries into wine.

DECIDUOUS

Pale flowers have a sickly fragrance

Each tiny flower has three to five petals

Soft and white in centre

Each stalk has two to four pairs of small leaflets with a single one at the tip

Small, shiny, black berries (fruit) on red stalks

Heavy clusters hang downwards

Each leaflet is oval in shape

COMPOUND

insects ○ birds ○ mammals ○ fungi ○ other . . . .

FACTFILE

Height 6–9 m

Where Widespread; parks, gardens

Flowering May/June

Fruiting September/October

Leaf tint/fall October–December

Other names Goldenchain, goldenrain

Uses Grown for ornament

PHOTOFILE

The buff-tip moth avoids predators by resting on a stem to look like a dried or broken twig. The yellow-black larvae of this moth feeds on the leaves of deciduous trees, including laburnum.

SEEN IT?

MY NOTES

Season:

Describe the tree:

Where is the tree?

What wildlife can you see?

How tall is your tree?

MEASURED IT?

STICK YOUR LEAF OR PHOTO HERE

On my tree I saw: leaves ○ buds ○ fruit ○ flowers ○

Laburnum *Laburnum anagyroides*

A common sight in British gardens, laburnum is recognisable by its cascades of bright-yellow flowers in the summer.

It originated in Europe and was introduced to Britain in the 16th century. All parts of the tree are poisonous, especially the seeds. The heartwood is deep brown in colour and was highly prized for making decorative items. It was often used as a substitute for the dark wood of the tropical ebony tree.

DECIDUOUS

Long spikes covered in many yellow flowers

Each hanging cluster of flowers is called a raceme

Grey-green, with soft hairs when young

Each leaf is made up of three leaflets

Seed pods (fruit) dry and open while still on the tree

Seed pods release black seeds that are very poisonous

Each leaflet is oval

COMPOUND

insects 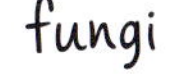 birds mammals fungi other . . . .

FACTFILE

Height 8–15 m

Where Widespread, mountains, parks, gardens

Flowering May

Fruiting October/November

Leaf tint/fall October/November

Other names Mountain ash, whispering tree, witchbane

Uses Bows, tool handles, bowls

PHOTOFILE

The ripening red berries of the rowan provide a feast for many birds, including the mistle thrush. These birds visit berry-laden trees in winter, and will often defend a tree from other birds.

SEEN IT?

MY NOTES

Season:

Describe the tree:

Where is the tree?

What wildlife can you see?

How tall is your tree?

MEASURED IT?

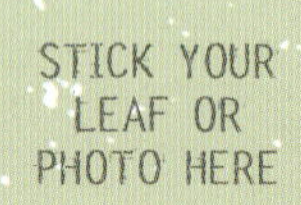

STICK YOUR LEAF OR PHOTO HERE

On my tree I saw: leaves ○ buds ○ fruit ○ flowers ○

Rowan *Sorbus aucuparia*

The magical rowan tree has a past steeped in history and mythology.

'Rowan' comes from the old Norse word for tree – *raun*. Its wood was used by druids to make their staffs and magic wands. People used to put sprigs of rowan in their houses to protect them from lightning, and sailors took it on board boats to protect them from storms. Raw berries are poisonous, but once cooked they can be eaten. As well as food and drinks, they have been used in herbal medicines.

DECIDUOUS

Fruits are orange-red berries up to 1 cm long

Fruits contain one or two seeds each

Purple-brown buds are covered in grey hairs

Small, creamy-coloured flowers grow in dense clusters

Each flower is 1 to 2 cm across

Each stalk has five to eight pairs of leaflets

Leaves change to golden orange and reddish-brown in autumn

insects  birds 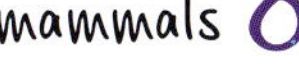 mammals  fungi  other . . . .

FACTFILE

Height 10–30 m

Where Southern England; woodland, parks

Flowering April–June

Fruiting September/October

Leaf tint/fall October/November

Other names Persian walnut, common walnut

Uses Furniture, veneers, nuts eaten as food

PHOTOFILE

Codling moths lay their eggs in June on the leaves or fruits of fruit trees, such as apple, pear and walnut. The larvae burrow into the fruit to eat. Once full, they eat their way out again.

SEEN IT?

MY NOTES

Season:

Describe the tree:

Where is the tree?

What wildlife can you see?

How tall is your tree?

MEASURED IT?

On my tree I saw: leaves ○ buds ○ fruit ○ flowers ○

Walnut *Juglans regia*

Walnut trees have been grown in Britain for their nuts, but also for their timber, which is one of the most beautiful woods in the world.

There is evidence that walnuts have been growing in Britain since at least Roman times, and they were widely planted in the 1800s. Thousands of walnut trees were felled in the Napoleonic wars so that the timber could be used to make guns for soldiers.

DECIDUOUS

Female flowers are small and green

Male catkins (flowers) grow up to 15 cm long

Hollow inside

Thick with a leathery surface

Fruits are round and green

An edible nut is inside the tough outer casing

Five to nine leaflets

COMPOUND

insects ○ birds ○ mammals ○ fungi ○ other . . . .

FACTFILE

Height 8–35 m

Where Widespread; parks, large gardens, churchyards

Flowering June–September

Fruiting August–October

Leaf tint/fall Evergreen

Other names Lebanese cedar

Uses Buildings, furniture

PHOTOFILE

Starlings are noisy, colourful birds that flock around tall trees, such as cedars. They nest in tree cavities, and often hop around the ground near tree roots searching for ants and other insects.

SEEN IT?

MY NOTES

Season:

Where is the tree?

Describe the tree:

What wildlife can you see?

How many hugs is this tree?

HUGGED IT?

Record your hug results at www.ancienttreehunt.org.uk

On my tree I saw: leaves ○ buds ○ fruit ○ flowers ○

Cedar of Lebanon *Cedrus libani*

This cedar is native to the mountain forests of the eastern Mediterranean, and has been a popular tree to plant in parkland and large gardens in the UK.

EVERGREEN

In ancient times, many of the cedar forests in Lebanon were felled to supply timber for building materials and fuel. Some stories tell of how it was first brought to Europe in the 18th century by a Frenchman, who uprooted a seedling while travelling in the Middle East. Not having a flowerpot he stored the young tree in his hat, looking after it until his return to Paris.

Male cones (flowers) are up to 8 cm long

Grey-green to yellow

Needles are up to 3 cm long

Large seed cones (fruit) ripen to brown

Often in tufts

Up to 15 cm long

NEEDLE

insects  birds mammals  fungi other ....

FACTFILE

Height 12–30 m

Where Widespread; woodland, parks, gardens, plantations

Flowering March/April

Fruiting September

Leaf tint/fall October/November

Other names Common larch

Uses Fences, furniture, boat building

PHOTOFILE

The common crossbill is a member of the finch family, often found near conifers such as larches. They make their nests out of twigs, moss, wool and hair. Crossbills eat conifer seeds.

SEEN IT?

MY NOTES

Season:

Where is the tree?

Describe the tree:

What wildlife can you see?

How tall is your tree?

MEASURED IT?

On my tree I saw: leaves ○ buds ○ fruit ○ flowers ○

European larch *Larix decidua*

Larches grow tall and straight and, unusually for conifers, they lose their leaves in the autumn.

These fast-growing trees produce good quality timber and they are often seen growing in plantations. In Siberia, it was once believed that man was created from a larch tree, and that woman was created separately from a conifer or fir tree. Herbalists use a weak tea made from the inner bark to treat stomach upsets and asthma.

DECIDUOUS

Seed cones (fruit) open to release seeds

Female flower is pink-red

Needles grow in bunches

Reddish brown bark

Male flowers are soft, yellow cones

Young needles

Up to 3 cm long

NEEDLE

insects ○ birds ○ mammals ○ fungi ○ other . . . .

FACTFILE

Height 20–50 m

Where Widespread; parks, grounds of historic buildings

Flowering May/June

Fruiting All year

Leaf tint/fall Evergreen

Other names Mammoth tree, Wellingtonia

Uses Leaves used in wreaths and floral displays

PHOTOFILE

Treecreepers have long toes that allow them to hang upside down and scuttle quickly up a tree's bark. They have brown and white mottled feathers, and are known to roost in sequoia trunks.

SEEN IT?

MY NOTES

Season:

Where is the tree?

Describe the tree:

What wildlife can you see?

How many hugs is this tree?

STICK YOUR LEAF OR PHOTO HERE

HUGGED IT?

Record your hug results at www.ancienttreehunt.org.uk

On my tree I saw: leaves ○ buds ○ fruit ○ flowers ○

Giant sequoia *Sequioadendron giganteum*

The giant sequoia is one of the tallest growing plants in the world and is also one of the longest living, capable of surviving up to 4000 years.

The tallest specimen is the General Sherman in the United States, which, in 1987, measured 83.8 m tall. Giant sequoias come from California and were brought to Britain in 1853, the year that the Duke of Wellington died. This is how this tree got its other name – Wellingtonia. The yew is one of few trees known to survive to a similar age.

EVERGREEN

Young seed cones (fruit) are green, maturing to brown

Up to 8 cm long

Small, green female flowers at tips of shoots

Scale-like leaves

Small, cone-like male flowers

Scales are pointed and overlappug

Yellow in colour and up to 1.5 cm long

NEEDLE

insects ○ birds ○ mammals ○ fungi ○ other . . . .

FACTFILE

Height 5–10 m

Where Mainly southern England; woodland, scrubland, chalky soils

Flowering May/June

Fruiting All year

Leaf tint/fall Evergreen

Other names Common juniper, dwarf juniper

Uses Wood used to smoke meat, fruits used to flavour gin

PHOTOFILE

The juniper carpet moth feeds mainly on juniper trees. These insects are only found in a few places in Britain and they are very well camouflaged. They fly from October to November.

SEEN IT?

MY NOTES

Season: ______

Where is the tree? ______

Describe the tree: ______

What wildlife can you see? ______

How many hugs is this tree? ______

STICK YOUR LEAF OR PHOTO HERE

HUGGED IT?

Record your hug results at www.ancienttreehunt.org.uk

On my tree I saw: leaves O buds O fruit O flowers 

Juniper *Juniperus communis*

RARE IN WILD

Juniper is a small, slow-growing, evergreen tree and can be found in a wide range of habitats all around the world.

Its fruits can take two to three years to ripen, so you may see black and green berries on the same tree. These are actually soft cones rather than true berries. As birds eat them and fly to other trees, they help distribute the seeds. In folklore, in parts of southwest England, the wood and needles were burned near a sick person and this was thought to cure infection.

EVERGREEN

Berry-like fruits take two to three years to ripen to black

Female flowers are tiny, green, scaly cones

Shoots are covered with slender, pointed needles

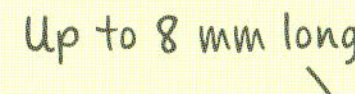

Male flowers are small, yellow cones

Needles grow in groups, or whorls, of three

NEEDLE

....

FACTFILE

Height 18–40 m

Where Widespread; plantations, parks

Flowering May

Fruiting September–November

Leaf tint/fall Evergreen

Other names Spruce fir

Uses Timber, paper, Christmas trees

PHOTOFILE

Coal tits are often seen near Norway spruces and other conifer trees. These tiny birds form large flocks in autumn and winter, in search of food, such as insects and seeds.

SEEN IT?

MY NOTES

Season:

Where is the tree?

Describe the tree:

What wildlife can you see?

How tall is your tree?

MEASURED IT?

STICK YOUR LEAF OR PHOTO HERE

On my tree I saw: leaves O buds O fruit O flowers O

Norway spruce *Picea abies*

It is believed that the Norway spruce was growing in Britain long before the last Ice Age.

This species did not return to Britain until around the 1500s when it was brought over from Europe. It is grown in plantations for timber and also for use as Christmas trees. The German tradition of decorating Christmas trees became fashionable in England in the 19th century after Queen Victoria married the German nobleman, Prince Albert.

Female flowers are reddish-brown and darken with age

Rough and scaly

Mature seed cones (fruit) are up to 17 cm long and hold many small seeds

Small male cones (flowers) grow close to the ends of shoots

Short, stiff needles grow in a spiral pattern

Reddish male cones turn yellow when pollen is produced

NEEDLE

insects ○ birds ○ mammals ○ fungi ○ other . . . .

FACTFILE

Height 12–36 m

Where Widespread; woodland, plantations

Flowering April

Fruiting April

Leaf tint/fall Evergreen

Other names Scots fir, giuis (Irish)

Uses Fences, flooring, telegraph poles, railway sleepers

PHOTOFILE

Wood ants live in colonies of up to half a million individuals. Some make their nests by piling up pine needles and other plant matter. They are reddish-brown in colour and up to 1 cm long.

SEEN IT?

MY NOTES

Season:

Where is the tree?

Describe the tree:

What wildlife can you see?

How many hugs is this tree?

HUGGED IT?

Record your hug results at www.ancienttreehunt.org.uk

On my tree I saw: leaves O buds O fruit  flowers O

Scots pine *Pinus sylvestris*

There are many conifers growing in Britain today, but the Scots pine is native to parts of Scotland, making it the only native British pine.

These fast-growing trees are found from Spain to Siberia. Scots pine trees grow tall and straight, and the wood is very hard-wearing, which makes it ideal for use as telegraph poles. Long ago, the wood was used in ship making and for water pipes. The cones have been used to forecast weather – it is thought that when the cones open the air is dry, so no rain should be expected.

EVERGREEN

CHAMPION TREE
MUIRWARD WOOD,
PERTH & KINROSS
GIRTH 628 cm

Small, yellow male cones (flowers) grow in groups

Long, slender needles up to 8 cm long

Red female flowers grown in pairs

Seed cones (fruit) are green at first, taking two years to ripen

Needles grow in pairs

Mature seed cones are woody and up to 7 cm long

NEEDLE

insects O birds O mammals O fungi O other . . . .

FACTFILE

Height 4–20 m

Where Widespread; churchyards, woodland

Flowering March/April

Fruiting October

Leaf tint/fall Evergreen

Other names Iur (Irish)

Uses Furniture, tool handles, an anti-cancer drug is made from the leaves

PHOTOFILE

Nuthatches are small birds with strong feet and ultra-sharp claws, and they are able to run head first down a tree trunk. They are one of many birds that may be seen in yew trees eating the fruits.

SEEN IT?

MY NOTES

Season:

Where is the tree?

Describe the tree:

What wildlife can you see?

How many hugs is this tree?

STICK YOUR LEAF OR PHOTO HERE

HUGGED IT?

Record your hug results at www.ancienttreehunt.org.uk

On my tree I saw: leaves ○ buds ○ fruit ○ flowers ○

Yew *Taxus baccata*

The dark, mysterious yew tree has been the subject of myths and legends for centuries, and it can often be found in cemeteries and church grounds.

Known to live for hundreds – sometimes thousands – of years, several churchyard yews are more than 1000 years old. In ancient times, people planted yews where they would be buried. Most parts of a yew tree are extremely poisonous to humans and animals.

EVERGREEN

CHAMPION TREE
ULCOMBE PARISH CHURCH,
KENT
GIRTH 990 cm

Needle-like leaves

Small male flowers turn yellow when they release pollen

Male flowers sit at the bases of leaves

Narrow, flat and dark green

Female flowers are tiny, green cones 1 to 2 mm long

Fruits are red, berry-like fruits, called arils

NEEDLE

insects ○ birds ○ mammals ○ fungi ○ other ....

Glossary

Bract A leaf-like part of a plant, found underneath a flower or its stalk.

Bud A rounded, undeveloped leaf or flower, often at the end of a twig or shoot.

Catkin A long, often hanging cluster of tiny flowers, on trees such as willows, oaks and birches.

Compound leaf A leaf made up of several smaller leaves called leaflets.

Coppice To cut back the stems of a tree to near ground level, causing many long, new shoots to grow up.

Cultivate To grow especially.

Deciduous Trees that drop their leaves every autumn.

Evergreen Trees that keep their leaves all year round.

Fruit The hard, soft or fleshy covering of the seed of flowering plants and trees.

Germinate To start to grow.

Girth The measurement around something, such as a tree trunk.

Hybrid A tree that is the offspring of two similar tree species eg the common lime.

Larva The worm-like young of an insect, eg a caterpillar, that changes into a winged, flying adult.

Leaflet A leaf or leaf-like section of a compound leaf.

Lobe A rounded part of a leaf that sticks out.

Native Originally from a particular country.

Pollard To cut back the top branches of a tree to encourage more to grow.

Scrubland An area of land, often covered with shrubs, bushes and grassland.

Shoot A new growth of a plant.

Acknowledgements

The publishers would like to thank the following artists who have contributed to this book:

Mike Foster, Andrea Morandi, Mike Saunders, Vivien Wilson

All other artworks from the Miles Kelly Artwork Bank

The publishers would like to thank the following sources for the use of their photographs:

Cover Andrew Bailey/FLPA; Page 4 Mike Alsford; 5(tl, ctr, cbl, br) WTPL/Pete Holmes; 6(c) Ancient Tree Hunt/Lorna Hall, (b) Ancient Tree Hunt/Katherine Owen; 7(l) WTPL, (r) WTPL; 9 WTPL; 12 Martin Garwood/NHPA; 14 Gail Johnson/Fotolia.com; 15(c) AndreyTTL/Fotolia.com, (r) Colin Varndell; 18 B. Borrell Casals/FLPA; 21(r) Colin Varndell; 22 Nigel Cattline/FLPA; 26 Harold Taylor/Photolibrary; 30 Bill/Fotolia.com; 31(r) Colin Varndell; 32 Stephen Dalton/NHPA; 33(r) Colin Varndell; 34 Tony Hamblin/FLPA; 35(r) Colin Varndell; 36 Sergey/Fotolia.com; 39(r) Colin Varndell; 44 G E Hyde/FLPA; 47(c) Robyn Mackenzie/Fotolia.com; 55(r) D.Harms/WILDLIFE/Still Pictures; 56 Tony Wharton/FLPA; 58 Tony Hamblin/FLPA; 62 Richard Becker/FLPA; 66 Robert Canis/FLPA; 68 Robert Canis/FLPA; 69(c) Roger Wilmshurst/FLPA, (r) Colin Varndell; 74 Tony Wharton/FLPA; 75(r) Colin Varndell; 78 Gary K Smith/FLPA; 79(c) Olena Kucherenko/Fotolia.com; 83(r) Colin Varndell; 86 Roger Wilmshurst/FLPA; 87(r) Colin Varndell; 88 Richard Becker/FLPA; 90 Martin B Withers/FLPA; 91(r) Colin Varndell; 94 John Hawkins/FLPA; 96 Nigel Cattlin/FLPA; 100 Martin Woike/Foto Natura/FLPA; 102 Derek Middleton/FLPA; 104 Joke Stuurman-Huiteman/Foto Natura/Minden Pictures/FLPA; 106 John Howkins/FLPA; 108 Robert Canis/FLPA

Poster (tr) Ancient Tree Hunt/Richard Littlewood, (tl) Ancient Tree Hunt/Dan Abrahams, (cr) Ancient Tree Hunt/David Martin, (cl) Ancient Tree Hunt/David Alderman, (bl) Ancient Tree Hunt/Ali Wright, (br) Ancient Tree Hunt/Peter Herring

All other photographs from:
Corel, digitalSTOCK, digitalvision, iStockphoto.com, John Foxx, PhotoAlto, PhotoDisc, PhotoEssentials, PhotoPro, Stockbyte, WTPL